MW00325807

The
Scarlet
Longing

RAHAB'S SECRET TO FINDING FREEDOM

A PROTOTYPE OF MERCY FOR RESCUE
AND HOPE FOR NEW BEGINNINGS

BRENDA D. VANWINKLE

Published by:
A Book's Mind in Partnership with Christian International
PO Box 272847
Fort Collins, CO 80527

Copyright © 2018
ISBN: 978-1-949563-06-1
Printed in the United States of America

Ancient Roots Linear Bible

Dedicated to every longing soul. He's on His way.

TABLE OF CONTENTS

Foreword   I
Prologue   V
Introduction   IX
Chapter 1: Looking Through Walls   1
Chapter 2: The Wooing   13
Chapter 3: The Breach   23
Chapter 4: The Strategies   35
Chapter 5: The Watchers   45
Chapter 6: The Circumcision   57
Chapter 7: The Sound and the Rescue   69
Chapter 8: The King and I   79
Afterward   91
Epilogue   97
Resource: Joshua 1-6   99

FOREWORD FOR
THE SCARLET LONGING

Rahab, the harlot. Tamar, a woman who played the harlot with her father-in-law, Judah. Bathsheba, the woman David committed adultery with and then murdered her husband. According to biblical culture and the religious norms of acceptability these women are to be considered tainted, shamed and rejected. However, it was these very women who found their way into the genealogy of Christ. The very bloodline of Jesus shows us that God has always desired to reach into the most desperate lives and broken hearts to display His goodness. Each of these stories showcase a beautiful picture of God's love and redemptive power to turn what seems to be cursed into a blessing. This is God's grace!

As a child who was not brought up to know the Lord, I discovered a deep longing inside to know the God I had only heard about. I saw depictions on television of people who would cry out to Him in times of trouble and then would receive answers to their prayers. I had no concept of my sin and how it separated me from God. I had no knowledge of a Savior who had given His life for me so that I could receive forgiveness. I had no framework to relate to how much the Father loved me and was longing to have relationship with me. But as empty as I was of head knowledge, my heart still yearned to know Him.

I spent hours on my knees (as I had seen on TV) crying out to a God I didn't know. I spent time every day reading a family Bible I discovered on a bookshelf, memorizing the prayers I found in the book of Psalms. Somehow, someway I knew I would find Him if I searched for Him with all my heart. Little did I realize He had already found me!

In *The Scarlet Longing,* Brenda Van Winkle invites us into the life of Rahab, the harlot, a woman full of sin and shame who longed for a different life and a new beginning. She had heard the stories of the God of Israel and of the many wonders He had worked on behalf of His people, the former Egyptian slaves. She felt enslaved herself and wondered if His power could possibly extend to her to give her a new start and a life of freedom as well.

Through this story of deciding to be on God's side, the salvation that was to follow and the fulfillment of dreams beyond her imagination, we find Rahab delivered from a life of sin and shame because she placed a scarlet cord in the window of her home that prevented her and her family from being destroyed with the rest of Jericho. She was then married to an Israelite of good standing and became the mother of a child named Boaz (of the book of Ruth). This positioned this once "lady of the night" to become the great, great grandmother of King David and later find herself in the genealogy of Christ, the Light of the world. She was not pure, she was not an Israelite, and by most standards she was not qualified for this honor. Yet God chose her and she chose Him and history was made.

In this book you will discover that each of us are actually a Rahab, trapped in sin and shame, not pure, not of the right bloodline and certainly not qualified to be one whom God would bless and use. But because the Father loved us and sent His son, Jesus, to take the penalty of our sin, His scarlet cord delivers us from doom and destruction and opens a whole new world to us of relationship with God and fulfillment of dreams. We are able to comprehend how our once tattered hearts can be transformed into lives of purity and purpose, much like that of the virtuous woman of Proverbs 31. It says of her "*Bold power and glorious majesty are wrapped around her as she laughs with joy over the latter days.*" *(vs 25).* This is how God sees His Bride, the Church. He delights in us and desires to wipe away our past pain and empower us with boldness and strength for the days ahead. As you read this amazing book, allow God's vision, purpose and destiny for your life to awaken the longing inside you for more of Him.

Dr. Jane Hamon
Apostle and Co-Pastor
Vision Church @ Christian International

PROLOGUE

I.

They Called Her Amber

Her dark eyes held secrets I didn't want to know. Those eyes had seen too much in the few years she had been alive, though what she had endured could hardly be called living. She sat there—small and slim and still. She could have hidden her gaze behind her long, straight black hair, but she didn't. She looked right at me, and I couldn't look away from her eyes—eyes filled with a story that longed to be expressed.

Our family had been serving in a restricted-access nation in Asia for many years. We had met many young women trapped in sex slavery. In their oppression, these women had quickly learned to read a foreigner's intentions just by looking into their eyes. Mostly, those intentions were awful. But sometimes, the women caught a glimpse of truth and hope and life. That's what we carried and why we were there, and that is what Amber wanted from me.

What she didn't want from me was my judgment or self-righteous offense. Yes, she had committed acts I did not want to know about. Yes, she had worshiped false gods as was common in her culture. And yes, she had even been trained as a killer, a terrorist, in fact. Three strikes and you're out.

Everything I knew about her made me want to turn away from the sin and perversion that had been her identity. I knew who and what she had been. I knew Amber was not the only name she had been called, though most likely it was the kindest. Any tiny bit of her story would disgust a good, moral person. And if she were to be found by the authorities, she and anyone colluding with her would have faced harsh questioning. Amber herself would face death. Looking into her eyes, I was aware some of what she lived through was worse than death.

What do we do in the face of such wickedness and sin? How are we, as carriers of God's love and presence, to respond? How do we handle our emotions and formulated ideas of what is worthy of love? Though we may think ahead of time that we always walk in love, when faced with a real person whose story is so completely other than our own, our heart has a choice to make.

This isn't an invented story designed to tug at your emotions. I met Amber. I looked in eyes that had seen sin like I never imagined. But as I looked at her, I also saw myself in a whole new way; I saw my preconceived judgments of others. I saw the way I ascribed them value or lack of value. I had many choices and heart changes to make. So do you.

We'll return to Amber's story later. But first, we have to travel back in time…and reposition our hearts.

II.

They Called her a Harlot

"Whore!"

Thousands of years have passed since she lived, yet when her name is mentioned even today, this most unsavory of descriptors is attached to it. I recently heard a pastor known for his kind heart speak of this woman from the Sunday morning pulpit with his lip curled in disdain: "Rahab the harlot," he spat. "The prostitute."

Something is very wrong with our heart attitude toward Rahab. And if toward Rahab—the fifth-great-grandmother of Jesus—then also toward women in general. And if toward women, then toward the Bride Jesus gave His life to spend eternity loving. If we are part of the Bride of Christ but we do not like or trust women, then we are double minded and unstable in all we do.

I've never heard Abraham's name spat out publicly—or anywhere else—as "Liar!" Nor Moses as "Murderer!" or David as "Sinner!" Even though Abraham lied, Moses murdered, and David's poor choices kept him from being permitted by God to build the temple, we no longer define these men by their sins. After God got ahold of their hearts and they turned to Him in repentance, we think of each of them by their redeemed identity: "Father of Faith!" "Deliverer!" "Man after God's own heart!"

It's time we give Rahab the same break--the same honor.

Yes, it is true that each time she is mentioned in the New Covenant she is called "Rahab the harlot." What if Holy Spirit was not trying to inspire us to look down on her for her pre-repentant life but instead reminding us that women, too, can be pulled from sin to salvation? That it's not OK to think there are levels of sin or variables in God's forgiveness? That just like he loves Abraham, Moses, and David, God also loves Rahab and sees her as His own?

Rest assured, your sins are not greater than those of these great men and women of old. Sin is the inheritance of all man through the first Adam, and it is the blood of the second Adam, Jesus, that makes us all clean before His Father, who is our God. When Jesus thinks of you, when heaven speaks your name, the adjectives used to describe you include:

Pure.
Spotless.
Bride.

Introduction

Our story begins in the Egyptian wilderness of Zin. Joseph, a son of Jacob (renamed "Israel" by God) and grandson of Abraham, was sold by his jealous brothers into slavery. He wound up in Egypt, serving in the household of the most powerful man on earth at that time: Pharaoh. Placed in a position of authority, Joseph paid attention to a pair of dreams Pharaoh had that warned of a coming drought and resulting famine. Joseph wisely began saving up a portion of each year's abundant grain crop so that when the foretold famine came, Egypt would have grain to keep itself and its neighboring nations alive.

Joseph's brothers, whose families were starving, traveled to Egypt to buy grain and there encountered their brother, Joseph, whom they presumed to be long dead. (I suggest you read the full and fascinating account of this historical event in Genesis 37-47). The family of Israel moved to the land of Goshen in Egypt. They prospered and became numerous just as the Lord had promised Abraham (Genesis 12:2, 22:17). As the Lord blessed the children of Israel with many children, the current Pharaoh, who didn't know of Joseph, became concerned that they were so numerous they posed a threat should they decide to rebel against him, so he enslaved them.

One day, a new king came to power *and ruled* over Egypt, but this king had no knowledge of Joseph.

Pharaoh *(to some of his advisors)*: Look! There are more Israelites than ever before, and they are *growing* more powerful than we are. We need to be careful in our dealings with them. Otherwise, they may grow even greater in number, and in a time of war join forces with our enemies, fight against us, and then leave the land.

So the Egyptian authorities *enslaved the Israelites and* appointed *cruel* slave drivers over them to oppress them with hard, *back-breaking* labor. They forced them to build the storage cities of Pithom and Raamses for Pharaoh. (Exodus 1:8-11 The Voice).

For 430 years, the children of Israel—known as Hebrews—were subjected to untold misery under this cruel bondage.

In the fullness of time, Moses was born as a slave to a Hebrew family. His birth came at a time when the Egyptians lived in dread of the children of Israel. The more the Egyptians afflicted them, the more they seemed to multiply, until Pharaoh ordered all male children to be killed at birth. When the Egyptian midwives refused to carry out this order, Pharaoh ordered that all male babies be thrown into the Nile River and drowned. A mass infanticide began. Moses' mother, desperate to save her baby, placed him in a basket and set it afloat in the Nile River, hoping and praying for the best. God heard her cry, and Moses—whose name means "drawn out of the water"—was saved when Pharaoh's daughter saw the basket, retrieved it, and drew Moses into the safety of her arms. How ironic that the very one Pharaoh meant to kill—the one who would deliver the Hebrews from his evil grasp—was now to be raised in his own home. Fed at Pharaoh's table, taught by the best warriors, wizards, strategists, and teachers available, Moses became second in line to the throne.

As a grown man, Moses killed an Egyptian and had to run for his life to the desert. There he learned a new set of lessons and a new way of life as he became a husband, a father, a son-in-law, and a shepherd. Moses seemed content with his new quiet life, away from the glamor and intrigue of the palace, but the Lord had not lost sight of this man He had chosen to deliver His people. Moses had an encounter with God in the wilderness that changed his life. He returned to Egypt where he did, indeed, lead his fellow Hebrews out of Egypt—out of slavery. They left captivity so that they could sacrifice to God; in other words, to freely worship Him. However, the stark reality of life in a desert soon brought out more whining than worship, more self-pity than praise, to the God of their forefathers.

They finally arrived at the border of Canaan, the land promised by God to be the fruitful, blessed inheritance of Abraham's descendants. Moses sent out twelve spies, one man from each of Israel's twelve tribes, to scope out Canaan and figure out how they might best claim their promise. Numbers 13:23 tells us that the spies came back with clusters of grapes so large, two men were required to carry them. Despite the fragrant and juicy visual aide they brought back, ten of the men could not see the large and fruitful abundance of the waiting Promised Land: all they could envision were the large Canaanite men they had seen. Giants, they called them. In fact, those ten spies said they felt as small as insects next to those Canaanite he-men. We will see later that the Canaanites were actually terrified of the Children of Israel. Only two of the twelve spies saw the Lord, the land, and themselves with eyes of faith: Joshua and Caleb. Despite these two men who championed going in and taking the land, the Israelites decided that going in to Canaan was just too much trouble—too risky. Because of their collective unbelief, the Lord declared that the nation would wander in the desert until that weary and faithless generation of former slaves was dead. Faith and courage would be required to take the inheritance God had for them, and this faith and courage would be found in a generation that had not known the fear, intimidation, and humiliation of slavery.

Joshua and Caleb had a new generation to mentor. They trained them with stories of God's faithfulness and miraculous interventions during the plagues that had come upon Egypt but not upon the Hebrews in Goshen; of the death angel that passed over the bright red lamb's blood painted over the doorposts of the Hebrew homes, showing a sacrifice had taken place to save them; of the dramatic intensity that built in each Hebrew heart as Pharaoh's pursuing army charged toward them, their whip-scarred backs now trapped up against an impassible Red Sea; of the faith of Moses who, at God's word, stretched out his staff so the sea parted and the Israelites walked through to the other side; of the cries of powerful Egyptian men and horses who started across the river in pursuit only to be drowned by the collapsing walls of water as they crashed and settled back into their banks. Over and over, the Israelites recounted stories of father Abraham, Isaac, and Jacob. Stories of bravery as well as tales of sin and defeat resounded as a generation counted and recounted the faithfulness of their God. Faith grew with each story told because faith comes through hearing. Courage fanned into flame as Joshua and Caleb told the young men of their ancestors' exploits with God, and the children played games by reenacting their forefathers' feats, not as slaves, but as heroes who walked with God.

Among the stories told were those of the Promised Land, of fruitfulness and an abundance of enticing food, flowing streams, and fertile land that awaited them there. The first year out of Egypt they longed for the onions of Egypt; by year 40 the children of the former slaves longed for the grain, figs, vines and pomegranates that awaited them in their promise. (Numbers 20:5). This generation knew they would need to deal with the giants and numerous warriors that were in Canaan, but they were also aware of the abundance God had in store; and for that, they now longed. Great fear accompanies great longing. Faith overcomes fear. And in the fullness of God's time, a generation was ready to go in and take their Promised Land. Their first stop was a Canaanite city called Jericho. God didn't start their Promised-Land journey by taking them in the back door to a small, unprotected village. Rather,

He marched His warriors straight toward the most depraved, wicked, and heavily fortified city in all the land. They began with Jericho. That is where I, too, begin to unravel the story of Jericho's most infamous citizen, Rahab.

Each chapter in this book begins with a portion of Scripture relevant to the events in that chapter. For your convenience, I have included the full story of Jericho as a resource at the end of the book, and I encourage you to re-read it if you haven't recently. It sets the stage for the scenes about to unfold.

In the midst of the horror of this evil city, God would once again free a slave. While the Hebrews were known as His children, this most unlikely heroine was destined to be a bride in Israel, one through whom the lineage of God's Son would come. Maybe God sent the nation of Israel first to Jericho because He couldn't wait another day to rescue Rahab, His beloved.

You will notice I have also included Proverbs 31 following this introduction. Proverbs 31 is the well-worn passage about the Virtuous Woman, the one we hate to love. What if she and Rahab are somehow connected? What if the Proverbs 31 passage actually *describes* Rahab—and you and me—as God sees both her and us? What if there is more to this journey of being His than we've yet known?

And so her story begins....

Proverbs 31

The Passion Translation

1 King Lemuel's royal words of wisdom: These are the inspired words my mother taught me.

2 Listen, my dear son, son of my womb. You are the answer to my prayers, my son.

3 So keep yourself sexually pure from the promiscuous, wayward woman. Don't waste the strength of your anointing on those who ruin kings— you'll live to regret it!

4 For you are a king, Lemuel, and it's never fitting for a king to be drunk on wine or for rulers to crave alcohol.

5 For when they drink they forget justice and ignore the rights of those in need, those who depend on you for leadership.

6-7 Strong drink is given to the terminally ill, who are suffering at the brink of death. Wine is for those in depression in order to drown their sorrows. Let them drink and forget their poverty and misery.

8 But you are to be a king who speaks up on behalf of the disenfranchised and pleads for the legal rights of the defenseless and those who are dying.

9 Be a righteous king, judging on behalf of the poor and interceding for those most in need.

The Radiant Bride

10 Who could ever find a wife like this one— she is a woman of strength and mighty valor! She's full of wealth and wisdom. The price paid for her was greater than many jewels.

11 Her husband has entrusted his heart to her, for she brings him the rich spoils of victory.

12 All throughout her life she brings him what is good and not evil.

13 She searches out continually to possess that which is pure and righteous. She delights in the work of her hands.

14 She gives out revelation-truth to feed others. She is like a trading ship bringing divine supplies from the merchant.

15 Even in the night season she arises and sets food on the table for hungry ones in her house and for others.

16 She sets her heart upon a nation and takes it as her own, carrying it within her. She labors there to plant the living vines.

17 She wraps herself in strength, might, and power in all her works.

18 She tastes and experiences a better substance, and her shining light will not be extinguished, no matter how dark the night.

19 She stretches out her hands to help the needy and she lays hold of the wheels of government.

20 She is known by her extravagant generosity to the poor, for she always reaches out her hands to those in need.

21 She is not afraid of tribulation, for all her household is covered in the dual garments of righteousness and grace.

22 Her clothing is beautifully knit together— a purple gown of exquisite linen.

23 Her husband is famous and admired by all, sitting as the venerable judge of his people.

24 Even her works of righteousness she does for the benefit of her enemies.

25 Bold power and glorious majesty are wrapped around her as she laughs with joy over the latter days.

26 Her teachings are filled with wisdom and kindness as loving instruction pours from her lips.

27 She watches over the ways of her household and meets every need they have.

28 Her sons and daughters arise in one accord to extol her virtues, and her husband arises to speak of her in glowing terms.

29 "There are many valiant and noble ones, but you have ascended above them all!"

30 Charm can be misleading, and beauty is vain and so quickly fades, but this virtuous woman lives in the wonder, awe, and fear of the Lord. She will be praised throughout eternity.

31 So go ahead and give her the credit that is due, for she has become a radiant woman, and all her loving works of righteousness deserve to be admired at the gateways of every city!

Chapter 1:
Looking Through Walls

*T*he citizens of Jericho had barricaded themselves behind its high walls because of the Israelite forces. No one could get in or out. Eternal One (to Joshua): I have given Jericho, its king, and all its soldiers into your hands. —Joshua 6:1-2 Voice

Since the rear wall of her house was actually part of the great city wall, she helped the men escape by simply lowering a rope for them from her window. —Joshua 2:15 Voice

She wraps herself in strength, might, and power in all her works.

She tastes and experiences a better substance, and her shining light will not be extinguished, no matter how dark the night. —Proverbs 31:17-18 TPT

If you can't see over the wall surrounding you, look through it.

Walls are built for protection. When storms come or an enemy attacks, secure walls provide us with invaluable protection and comfort. But if we are trapped inside the walls, they become not only obstacles to freedom, but they also start to feel suffocating, limiting us physically and mentally.

For those of us who have been raised in the typical traditions of western Christianity, the walls surrounding us are as varied as the people who built them. Some of our walls are simple and plain, others are ornate. Within one set of walls, one might find quiet contemplation, and in another, one might find high-decibel worship music. Regardless of the scene within them, churches are built with walls that keep us safe and together when we gather. As wonderful and beautiful as the varied expressions of worship are, we often forget to look out the Church window at the world around us, thereby keeping our worldview trapped within walls of familiar tradition and our own inner need for security and safety.

If you can't see over the wall, look through it.

In 2012 I published a book called *An Unclouded Sun,* based on the story of Deborah in Judges 4-5. As a woman who saved her nation from terrorism, the premise of the book was timely; earlier in the year of publication, Osama bin Laden was killed by US troops in Afghanistan.

My sister's name is Deborah, and I had dedicated the book to her. Of course I hoped she liked the book—I wanted her to be honored and pleased. She seemed to be, but rather than gushing about it and feeding my ego, she said to me, "Now you need to write a book about Rahab."

"Rahab?" I asked. "I don't know anything about her."

To which Debbie quipped, "I don't either. That's why you need to write a book."

Whether I liked it or not, her words struck a deep chord in me that has continued to resonate until this day. Over the last few years, I've found myself drawn to the story of Rahab in the Book of Joshua, and I have been reading it over and over. Her story races through my head. I wake up in the night with questions about her life as I ponder this most unlikely candidate for salvation and promotion. Yet the Lord did not consider her unworthy of salvation or promotion, quite the opposite. She was not only saved from the destruction of Jericho but also married a Hebrew man and became part of the lineage of Jesus the Messiah. Surely there is more to her story than I've seen through my religious walls! Surely there is a window—a crack in the wall of my defenses—through which I can see to unlock a mystery that has surrounded this woman we have loved to hate for a very long time.

Through years of asking the Lord about her and listening to His whispers of revelatory wisdom, my way of seeing her story has opened wide a window of hope and a path of freedom for all who are willing to look--to *see*; for all who have the courage to change their inside-the-walls thinking and look again.

What if we could leave our own Jerichos and enter into freedom we never thought could be ours?

When Our Eyes Get Slammed Open

Though our family had been serving in Southeast Asia for a number of years, our eyes got slammed open to the world of prostitution and sex trafficking in the late 1990s. It seemed to be increasing. Red light districts, advertised by the dim pink lights displayed in shop windows, became both more common and obvious. Scantily clad, heavily made-up young women began loitering more and more in hotel lounges, and whispers of AIDS were heard. Near where we lived was a large garbage heap. More than once, we saw used needles tossed among the refuse. And more than once, we witnessed small children playing with those needles, laughing and pretending.

On our return trips to the States, we would share what we were seeing in Southeast Asia with people and churches. At that time, no one used the terms "human trafficking" or "sex trafficking." And in our polite Christian circles, it seemed like no one *wanted* to know about them. There was simply no grid at the time for the North American Church to comprehend that this was happening.

During those years, I was invited to host a table at a large conference in Texas. My husband, Jim, and I had brought back jewelry made by girls who had been rescued from prostitution. Though this has become common now, at the time it was a new concept. Jim and I would purchase as much jewelry as we could from the girls, bring it back to the States to sell at churches when we spoke, and then take the funds back to the girls to buy supplies to make more jewelry and build better lives for themselves.

We had come face to face with the dark world of trafficking in Asia, but I remember my shock and disbelief when I heard about it happening in our own country. After I spoke at the conference in Texas, people stopped by our table to ask questions and then, as they left, looked over their shoulders before whispering, "You know it's happening right here in America, right?" A Californian told us that the largest ring in the US was in California along I-5. Then someone from Arkansas stopped by and told us the largest ring was in Little Rock. The Washington D.C. resident whispered that D.C. has the highest rate, and so on. Suddenly, the lid cracked open to give us a peek into the darkness in this land, and our eyes were opened once again.

In the years since the 1990s, this dark web of perversion has grown; thankfully, so has our corporate awareness of it. And with awareness, prayer and intercession has increased to the point that exposure and justice are soon to be forthcoming. As this happens, will we know how to respond to the survivors in love? How will we, as God's children, view those who have lived opposite to the tenants of our faith? How will we see them, and how will our vision affect our response to them? May our new look at Rahab grant us a prototype of mercy for rescue and hope for new beginnings.

The Other Woman

If Rahab is the woman we love to hate, the Bible also presents us with a woman we hate to love: the "virtuous woman" of Proverbs 31. I know I am not the only person who has wondered what this woman is even doing in the Bible! After all, Jesus is our only standard of perfection, so why does the Proverbs 31 woman present an unattainable, unrealistic standard?

What if she, too, is more than the label she has been given?

Every time I would refuse to think about Rahab for another minute, Proverbs 31 would come stand right in the middle of my spiritual sight. I soon realized that Holy Spirit was not only directing me to both of these women but perhaps had woven a cord of truth connecting them.

I love "God puzzles." I love how He reveals pieces of revelation and understanding that shape the treasures He has hidden for us— even when we have no clue what those treasures are. Unlike a jigsaw puzzle, these revelatory puzzles come together as we look beyond the walls of our familiar worldview.

Unpacking Proverbs 31

As I studied this chapter, something began to bother me. Why is it that most every translation divides it into two distinct parts? Was it originally written that way or were the divisions added later? The chapter begins with a warning to King Lemuel (universally accepted to be King Solomon) about women and wine. He is warned that there are women who destroy kings (verse 3) and that drinking can cause a king to forget what has been decreed and pervert the rights of the afflicted (verses 3-5). We are not told who these afflicted ones are.

Interestingly, this chapter reads like a page lifted from the king's journal with a heading that could easily have been: "Things My Mom Said I Should Do and Not Forget". Who advises kings? In this case, the king's mother. If the king is Solomon, the mother is Bathsheba: a woman who was not initially protected but rather violated and made a widow by a king—King David. (You can read this story in 2 Samuel 11.) She became a good and loyal wife to this man David whose heart was after God. She instructs her son, who becomes king, how to protect both himself and those in his kingdom. It is not defined whether this instruction is for men or women; in the first part the pronoun "he" is used, but the second half speaks of a woman, so both genders are included. (And it is possible that the exclusivity of male in the first part and female in the second is more a matter of the writer's stylistic choice than it is a restriction limited to gender.)

Perhaps verse 10 lends us some insight. Without headings and breaks, the very next instruction the king's mama gives him is about a wife. A wife? Wait a minute. We've just read verse after verse about unidentified poor, destitute, voiceless, nameless subjects in his kingdom. And then begins the famous verses about wives and women—verses that have historically been used as a weapon *against* women who cannot possibly live up to these standards; verses that women have used against themselves as proof of their own unworthiness. The final chapter of the Book of Proverbs ends by describing a superwoman, wife, and daughter.

Bathsheba had been the wife of a loyal man, only to have the King David impregnate her and then—after learning she was expecting a royal child—to have her husband killed. It is not hard to imagine her feeling voiceless and powerless regarding the choices being made for her life by another.

I am a mother of four children, including a son. Proverbs 31 begins by telling us that the things written within are what King Lemuel's mother taught him. If I did give my son pre-marital advice, I'm sure it did not sound like this. But this woman is the queen and her son has both authority and responsibility to care for those under his rule. What if, as a mom, she uses this chat with him to describe the plight of women and men before they have a rescuer? What if she is proposing the wide-open possibilities available to them as a result of being saved? What if the Proverbs 31 woman was never about one single, solitary woman but about a mysterious, supernatural entity comprised of both men and women who would—who *could*—fulfill the multiple high standards listed here?

This, indeed, is what a pure, spotless Bride would look like for a King who would speak for the voiceless, who would offer the wine of hope to the desperate, and who would judge righteously. This King would deserve a virtuous wife more valuable than rubies. Suddenly the Proverbs 31 woman becomes not an unattainable standard that has been set which no mere human can ever attain, but rather a collective reality of what the people of God, rescued from their own Jericho, look like when the King calls them by name.

Back To Rahab

As I continued thinking about Rahab, pursuing the depths of her story, I began to feel myself becoming her advocate. As often happens, once you focus on something, you begin hearing about it everywhere. This happened with me regarding Rahab—but not in a good way. What I heard hurt my heart. Pastor after pastor, speaker after speaker, and blog after blog referred to her with disgust and distain.

But wait. Despite who she was and the life she lived, the God of the Hebrews—our Redeemer—saw fit to rescue her when everyone else in her entire city, except her family, was brutally wiped out. As if that were not enough, she was then so transformed, she married well in Israel. Her husband would have been from the tribe of Judah because she became the fifth-great grandmother of Jesus, who would break down walls and save all who would follow Him.

Romans 1 and 2 tells us not only what God considers sin and depravity but also the fact that not one of us is without sin. As I read the list of sins in Romans 1, it can be easy to feel like I am off the hook—I never murdered anyone. Or have I? Jesus got right to the heart when He said if I have been angry with someone, I am judged the same as if I have murdered (Matthew 5:21-22). Ouch. Perhaps you don't remember ever being angry without a genuine cause toward anyone? Well done! But have you ever whispered something about someone that you would not have said to his or her face? Yes, "whisperer" is included in that list of sins in Romans 1:29. In fact, Romans 2 begins, "Therefore you are inexcusable, O man, whoever you are who judge, for in whatever you judge another you condemn yourself; for you who judge practice the same things" (NKJV).

In other words, author Paul makes it clear in Romans 3:23 that we *all* have sinned and fallen short of the glory of God. I guess you could say we have each been Rahab. What? You have never prostituted yourself? That is wonderful. But remember, Romans 1 lays a level playing field, making us aware that sin is sin is sin. Not one of us has been the Proverbs 31 woman and lived in total victory and freedom. But we have each been Rahab. And as we humble ourselves, as we allow Holy Spirit to throw open the window so we can see beyond the walls of our previous understanding and lead us out and into a wide-open Promised Land, we will collectively become the Bride.

You see, it is not about owning your own land or weaving your own scarf from the wool of sheep you raised and sheared yourself—spinning your own yarn to boot. I *have* "bought a field"; I have given years of my life to serve the unreached in other nations. Many of you have also, as you taught Sunday School or reached out to the poor in your neighborhood, or have been foster parents. I *have* "spun wool"; I find great warmth and comfort and can spread it over others I meet to warm them, too, from the lessons I have learned and gathered while being a mother not only to my four birth children but a spiritual mother to children all over the globe. Many of you have done the same. You have a photo on your refrigerator of the child in another nation you support with finances and prayer each month. Or, as a doctor, you have given of your time and resources to serve in the inner city and hold free clinics. We have all been "spinning wool" much longer than we know.

Throwing Open The Window

A worldview is often determined by what we experience. Rahab's world expanded beyond the infamous window in her upstairs room, which gave her a view *out* of Jericho. All it takes is an outward look to change the way we see and perceive, to increase our awareness and faith so that what we believe becomes real and possible.

2 Chronicles 16:9a says, "For the eyes of the Lord run to and fro throughout the whole earth, to show Himself strong on behalf of those whose heart is loyal to Him" (NKJV).

The Lord was looking for Rahab in Jericho. He was looking for one person of faith He could count on in the midst of Jericho's depravity. He looked for her before she knew to look for Him, but her eyes were open, and she did not miss her chance. And that made all the difference.

King Lemuel was instructed to defend women because the scarlet thread woven throughout the biblical narrative is the coming of the Messiah and the preparation of His Bride. And if about a Bride, then it is about men as well as women, for together we comprise the Bride of Christ.

If you closely read the stories of Rahab and the Proverbs 31 woman, you will see a wealth of similarities. Each woman:

- Delights in work of her hands
- Stewards wealth and has multiple streams of income
- Defends truth
- Exhibits strength and valor in times of war
- Is in just the right place at just the right time
- Possesses faith that overcomes circumstances
- Breaks through the restrictions of her role in society
- Is destined for royalty
- Leaves a legacy of kings
- Operates with wisdom
- Is safe and trustworthy
- Brings good not evil
- Seeks wool and flax
- Brings food from afar
- Intercedes and watches over her family
- Plants a vineyard (which can also be interpreted as setting her heart on a nation)
- Stretches out her hand to her distaff
- Not afraid of snow (unafraid of tribulation)
- Knows the value of scarlet cloth
- Makes clothing for herself, her family, and to sell

- Clothes herself in strength and honor
- Marries into a powerful family
- Is fearless about the future and rejoices at what is to come
- Is wise and kind
- Is blessed by her children
- Is praised by her husband
- Lives in fear, wonder, and awe of the Lord
- Will be praised throughout eternity

Only one "woman" can, should, and will fulfill all of this: the Bride of Christ.

Questions for Consideration

Victims feel they have no voice, and shame empowers a victim mentality. When you read stories of women who lived lives of sexual perversion and of the men who used and abused them, shame can arise from a totally different area in your life. Shame wraps around emotions. When you begin to move toward freedom, shame acts like a python and squeezes until it takes your breath away. As your perspectives are challenged and your emotions stirred, be aware of God's presence. Feel His pleasure over you. You are an overcomer, not a victim. I bless you with the courage to believe that and to walk away from all that restricts you from your future. Breathe freely!

1. What are the first three words that come to mind when you hear the name Bathsheba?
2. Are you surprised at those words? Why or why not?
3. What kinds of emotions arise when you think of the Proverbs 31 woman?
4. Have you ever stopped to think that Bathsheba is likely the author of Proverbs 31?
5. Considering this, is there any action your heart needs to take? Maybe repentance (which is to change the way your thoughts

were taking you)? Maybe the willingness to allow God to open your heart to be less hasty to judge?

6. If we have been so quick to judge those who lived long ago and are in the lineage of Jesus, how quick are we to judge one another today?

A Blessing

Be blessed by this truth: it is safe to let go of the fear that has disabled your heart from being able to trust. Rahab was in a horrible life situation yet she was kept by the One for whom her heart longed. May you allow your heart to let go of the judgments you have made against yourself and others. May Holy Spirit break shame off your life and enable you to step into bold courage. May you find your voice so that, like Rahab, you can speak His wonders. I speak freedom to your spirit, soul, and body to know you are secure in His heart. May the deep rest that comes from knowing you belong in His heart enable you to make a fresh, new start as an overcomer. You've got this and He's got you.

CHAPTER 2:
THE WOOING

...the two men lay where she had hidden them beneath the stalks of flax laid out on her roof.

Rahab: I know the Eternal has given your people this land. Your coming has paralyzed us all with fear. We have heard how the Eternal held back the Red Sea so you could escape from Egypt on dry land and how you completely destroyed the Amorite kings, Sihon and Og – and their kingdoms – on the far side of the Jordan. As soon as this news reached us, our hearts melted like wax and none of us had an ounce of courage left. The Eternal One, your God, is truly God of the heavens above and the earth below. —Joshua 2:6b, 9-11 Voice

She sets her heart upon a nation and takes it as her own, carrying it within her. She labors there to plant the living vines. —Proverbs 31:16 TPT

Turn Around, Look At Me

On a recent trip to Dublin, Ireland, my husband and I found ourselves having breakfast and coffee on the patio of Malahide Castle. Across the beautiful grounds, a male peacock began a loud, brash squawking that clashed with his outward finery. He made his way across the lawn near to where we were sitting. He wasn't interested in us though. He was interested in the peahen who strolled by in haughty nonchalance. The peacock threw out his chest and began strutting as though he were king. He shook his tail and his feathers began rising in a majestic display of color and intricate beauty. By this point, everyone on the patio had already raced to the wall with cell phone cameras to take a video or snapshot of his grand performance. There were "ooohs" and "aaahs" in abundance and much talk of his magnificence. The only one who didn't seem to notice or care was the object of his wooing: the peahen. She maintained her cool and her distance and acted as though she didn't know he existed. All that work for so little interest! But that was just on the surface. Underneath her cool exterior was, I suspect, a little peahen heart delighting in the attention and bravado being displayed just for her.

How we all, humans and animals alike, long to be wooed to love.

Longing

What does the Bible say about people longing to be wooed, to be loved, by God? Let's look at a few Scriptures....

Proverbs 8:17 in the Ancient Roots Translinear Bible:

"I love my lovers anticipating me and finding me."

Imagine! Jesus, King of all Kings, loves when people anticipate and find Him.

Psalm 33:17-22 in the The Passion Translation:

Human strength and the weapons of man are false hopes for victory; they may seem mighty but they will always disappoint. The eyes of the Lord are upon even the weakest worshipers who love him—those who wait in hope and expectation for the strong, steady love of God. God will deliver them from death, even the certain death of famine, with no one to help.The Lord alone is our radiant hope and we trust in him with all our hearts. His wrap-around presence will strengthen us.As we trust, we rejoice with an uncontained joy flowing from Yahweh!Let your love and steadfast kindness overshadow us continually, for we trust and we wait upon you!

That speaks for itself.

Romans 1:11 in the New King James Version:

"For I long to see you, that I may impart to you some spiritual gift, so that you may be established...."

Paul, the author, writes to his friends in Rome that he longs to see them. Another way to translate this is: I *yearn* to be with you. Yearn is a word of strong emotion, desire that turns one inside out. Longing and yearning are not only part of our experience as people toward one another but are also healthy and natural expressions of our love for God. In fact, He loves it when we long for Him. Rahab, despite living a life of sin, was not consumed by that sin; rather, her longing for and hope in the God of Israel caught His attention and captured His heart.

Rahab in Jericho

It would be difficult to overstate the depravity that was part of the everyday life of the residents of Jericho. The Bible does not speak of any righteous within the walls. Remember Sodom? Even in that city of evil, there was one righteous man: Lot. There was not even one in Jericho. But there was one – a 'woman of the night' – who longed to live in the freedom of God's daylight, whose heart desired to be righteous. He who would one day come in the flesh to seek and save the lost knew she was there and came to her rescue.

Before Jesus came in human flesh, the Lord's command to His people was always to keep themselves away from the sinfulness of the nations that surrounded them. Not only did He want them to keep His commands—given in love to protect them—He also wanted to keep pure the line through which Messiah would come. When God sent His people to take possession of the Promised Land of Canaan, there were to be no compromises. Though it seems overbearing to our twenty-first-century minds, the Lord Himself commanded that entire people groups be removed from the Promised Land. This was not only as a judgment of their sin against Him but also as a means of securing the nation against further depravity. Jericho was no exception.

It can be a challenge to read the historical accounts of Jericho. All the sin and wickedness! As in many such cultures, the weakest members were offered as sacrifice to appease the whims of false gods. Temple prostitution and child sacrifice were commonplace. To visit a temple prostitute was considered a way to gain favor with the gods. It would be hard to exaggerate the evil of the city of Jericho. Imagine being a woman or child in a city where the walls surrounding you did not protect but rather trapped you. I cannot comprehend what living in such a world does to the psyche. It causes humans to live more like animals.

But sometimes, beyond all likelihood, there is one who dares to find an opening and look out through a wall they cannot climb--like Rahab.

Her Way of Life

Was Rahab a prostitute? Undoubtedly. The Bible calls her that in more than one place. And to be a prostitute in Jericho meant that she would have been involved in some of the most perverted sexual and societal practices in history. But she was more than her actions, and sometimes we forget that. In Matthew 1, Holy Spirit goes out of the way to honor her by name in the lineage of Jesus, and the author of Hebrews lists her with the heroes of faith in chapter 11.

Who is this woman? In addition to being a prostitute, she may have also been an innkeeper; the fact that the two spies Joshua sent into Jericho stayed with her hints at this. We don't know that for sure but, at any rate, she had a home located on the wall of Jericho to which people came. Was it strictly to take part as a client in her prostitution? Perhaps. Perhaps not. Either way, she seems to have known how to run a business and handle money—and men.

I also suspect she was a businesswoman because of the linen laid out on the roof of her house, which she used to hide the spies. Perhaps Rahab owned a field and had workers or family that harvested flax used to make linen. Perhaps she was a spinner of thread and made linen, or a weaver who created tapestries and clothing for her household. Whatever her work, she had lengths of linen on her rooftop as well as a linen rope or cord dyed red in her home.

The Yearning

What caused Rahab to take up prostitution? I don't know that any more than I know why I hate or covet or cheat. Many books and novels have been written embellishing the story of what caused her to take this destructive path. While they are interesting and entertaining, I'm not as interested in her downfall as I am her redemption. Remember, we all have fallen short of God's glory, and each of us has the same sin nature as Rahab until Jesus rescues us. My question therefore is: what great faith did it take for Rahab to live in Jericho, deal daily with its wickedness, and never stop longing for the One she heard about through stories whispered about town, this God of the Hebrews who forbade child sacrifice and temple prostitution because of love? This God who went out into the desert and rescued Hagar and her son, honoring and elevating women beyond any man she had yet encountered?

It seems inevitable that Rahab met more than one man in her life who, like the peacock, strutted his tail feathers and made a good showing of his prowess, who spoke words of interest and affection that sounded like intolerable lies to her jaded ears. Defying all odds, Rahab chose to look outward from Jericho toward the Hebrew camp, aching with everything in her to meet this One; to know and be known by the One greater than a man, who could speak true words of true love, One whose very presence would both free and captivate the captive. Like you, like me, Rahab needed to be loved and to belong in a safe place. Though she and we may not feel worthy of being loved, we acknowledge that such love is what we need most, and that God is the one who will never disregard or disparage us. How could one not long for such a Man as this?

Bringing It Home

Again we look to the Scriptures and are reminded: For the eyes of the Lord run to and fro throughout the whole earth, to show Himself strong on behalf of those whose heart is loyal to Him (2 Chronicles 16:9a NKJV).

God was looking for Rahab, just as today He continues to look for me, for you. She was the one person of faith He could count on in the midst of Canaanite depravity. Like righteous Noah before her, she became righteous by loving Him, and her righteousness saved her family from the total destruction of her city. As I mentioned before, God looked for her before she knew to look for Him.

I was raised in a Christian home and came to know Jesus at an early age. However, by age eighteen, I was desperately longing for more. Though I searched to find an easing of this inexplicable yearning in my soul, all I found was the status quo, and that was not enough. One night, in total desperation, I stood at the window of my bedroom, looked up to the sky, and said out loud to this God I ached to know and be known by, "God, I want everything you are. I love you, I need you. I must have this thing I don't know how to define. If you are who I believe you to be, I'm asking you to meet with me and come rescue me. And if you are not, then you are a small and disappointing god who I've already reached the limits of, so this is good bye." From this, you might get the impression that I was puffed up in my perceived maturity or disrespectful to speak in such a way to the Lord. In truth, I was neither. I was simply undone by my deep hunger to experience firsthand more of who He is, and He was neither surprised nor put off by my honest cry. How many, how very many, of us have cried out, "If you are who you say you are, come rescue me!" It is a cry He cannot and will not ignore.

Walls Cannot Stop Love

He has made everything beautiful in its time. Also He has put eternity in their hearts... —Ecclesiastes 3:11a NKJV

The name Rahab means conqueror. And what a lot she had to conquer! Even while living in depraved Jericho, Rahab found the eternity God placed in her heart. The heart of a prostitute could easily have been a heart of stone, yet hers was softened by one glance of His mercy. Even the physical stones of Jericho presented no obstacle to the One True God whose very name is Love. No matter what we have done, Rahab's life testifies to the truth that when we align with God and leave our past behind, that past—when repented of and forgiven—is washed away, and our future becomes secured with hope. What a display of grace.

Jericho was Rahab's Promised Land as well as that of the Hebrews. She first had to see outside of its confinement--the prison that sin had formed as walls around her. Once faith walked her into freedom, she would find her tribe, her true home. Jericho was too small for her destiny. Her future was as broad and spacious and abundant as the land and promise of Canaan.

Displacing Fear

There is no fear in love; but perfect love casts out fear...—1 John 4:18a NKJV.

As she saw the Israelites advancing on her city, she and her fellow residents knew Jericho was doomed. Who could stand against this God who did wonders?

Faith is the antithesis of fear. Rahab's faith was profound, especially considering that what she knew about God was based on rumors which were, in turn, based on the fear of her fellow townspeople.

It is a scary prospect to consider joining another tribe—to consider being an outsider, yet, in many ways, Rahab was already an outsider in her own hometown. By faith and the kindness and mercy of God, she became an insider in Israel, and she stands as a testimony of hope to all who are lost and long for more of His presence. An entire city saw the Israelite enemy coming and prepared for battle. Rahab saw God coming and prepared for the victory of a fresh start, a new beginning. Rahab's thoughts about God were more accurate than the Israelites'—God's own people, whom He had led out of Egypt. Her thoughts were more accurate than my own thoughts sometimes are.

Brian Simmons says it well: "Jesus is everything that righteousness stands for. He is the perfect example of manhood, perfection, grace, and uprightness. Those who are upright in heart will see in Him their perfect model and spouse."

Questions for Consideration

Genesis 1:26-28 and 2:18 tell us the original intention of God for man and woman. He blessed them with a sacred call and destiny as well as a complementary uniqueness to one another. He walked with man and woman—a three-strand cord—as their lives wrapped around His presence. Love, Himself, chose to be with them and honored them with His nearness.

To be valued and celebrated are two of our most basic, God-given longings. When we are in right relationship with Him, at home in His presence, these longings are satisfied.

Proverbs 31 is written about a woman and corresponds to Psalm 112, which is written about a man. They are remarkably similar passages that describe the company of the Bride: not an exclusive male or female company, but an expression of unity, of being His.

1. What does your heart long for?
2. What seems to stand in your way of seeing that longing fulfilled?
3. Of what are you most afraid?
4. What keeps you from drawing near to Him?
5. Take time to read Psalm 112 with Proverbs 31 in mind. God created man and woman individually and uniquely for individual and unique roles, though we were meant to live in unity, in one-ness. What do the similarities between Psalm 112 and Proverbs 31 say to you about the Bride of Christ?
6. Take a moment and ask Holy Spirit how He would have you respond to His wooing. Allow Him to renew you and give you hope.

A Blessing

I bless you with the words of Brian Simmons, author of The Passion Translation, as written in the footnote of Proverbs 31:10. Allow these truths and the power of revelation to walk your heart into freedom:

> The Hebrew word used to describe this virtuous wife is *chayil*. The meaning of this word cannot be contained by one English equivalent word. It is often used in connection with military prowess. This is a *warring wife*. *Chayil* can be translated, "mighty; wealthy; excellent; morally righteous; full of substance, integrity, abilities, and strength; mighty like an army." The wife is a metaphor for the last days' church, the virtuous, overcoming bride of Jesus Christ. The word *chayil* is most often used to describe valiant men.

May we be valiant men and women, the Bride of Christ, walking together in a unity secured by the Bridegroom's blood. He has fulfilled our deepest longings.

CHAPTER 3:
THE BREACH

*T*hen Joshua, the son of Nun, secretly sent two spies from Shittim to the western side of the Jordan.

Joshua: Go in, and see what you can find out about the people in that area. Pay special attention to the city of Jericho.

The men crossed the river, and when they entered Jericho, they stayed at the home of a prostitute named Rahab.

Somehow word reached the king of Jericho that Israelite spies had slipped into the area and might be visiting Rahab. That night the king sent soldiers to Rahab's house with a message.

Messengers: The king commands you to turn over the Israelite men who are staying with you because they are there to spy on all the land and its defenses.

But Rahab had already hidden the two spies before she received the king's messengers.

Rahab: It's true that two men have been to see me. But I didn't take the time to ask them where they came from. All I know is that when it was getting dark outside and the gate was about to close, they got up and left. I don't know where they went from here. If you hurry, you might still catch up to them.

She was lying, because the two men lay where she had hidden them beneath the stalks of flax laid out on her roof.
—Joshua 2:1-6 Voice

She searches out continually to possess that which is pure and righteous. She delights in the work of her hands.

...

Even in the night season she arises and sets food on the table for hungry ones in her house and for others.

...

She stretches out her hands to help the needy and she lays hold of the wheels of government.— Proverbs 31:13,15,19 TPT

An Opening Gives Access

A breach is an opening—a gap in a wall or boundary. It is a term often used to describe the offensive action of an invading army. A breach allows access where there previously was none. The opening, once formed, allows not only those on the outside to get in but also those trapped on the inside to get out. Sometimes a breach is large and obvious. Other times it is as simple as sticking one's foot in an open door so it cannot close.

Interestingly, Joshua only sent in two spies to explore Canaan—specifically, Jericho's defenses. Remember that Moses sent in twelve spies for the original reconnaissance. Despite coming home with abundance and bounty, ten of the twelve returned in fear. The scripture reads like this:

Then they [the ten spies] told him [Moses], and said, "We went to the land where you sent us. It truly flows with milk and honey, and this is its fruit. Nevertheless the people who dwell in the land are strong; the cities are fortified and very large; moreover we saw the descendants of Anak there".... But the men who had gone up with him [Caleb] said, "We are not able to go up against the people, for they are stronger than we." And they gave the children of Israel a bad report of the land which they had spied out, saying, "The land through which we have gone as spies is a land that devours its inhabitants, and all the people whom we saw in it are men of great stature. There we saw the giants (the descendants of Anak came from the giants); and we were like grasshoppers in our own sight, and so we were in their sight." (Numbers 13:27-28, 31-33 NKJV)

The two of twelve who came back with faith—ready to obey God and take the land—were the two who were still alive after the exodus from Egypt: Joshua and Caleb. All the rest of the men who left Egypt died in the wilderness because of their fear and doubt and unbelief. Joshua was now leader of Israel along with Caleb, his right-hand man. Perhaps remembering this former time of shame and frustration, (after all, he and Caleb were ready to take Canaan forty years ago), Joshua sent in just two men. In chapter two we read that when they arrived in Jericho they went to Rahab's house and lodged there for the night. This action, staying at Rahab's, became the breach, the opening, the entry point through which the unfolding plans of God would now weave.

Another Example of Breaching

Judah is the name of one of the sons of Israel. He and his wife (who, like Rahab, was a Canaanite) had a son named Er. Judah later gave Er a wife named Tamar. Er died and Tamar had the misfortune to be passed down the line to Judah's second son, who died leaving no heir.

Judah then promised Tamar to his third son, Shelah. This was done according to the law, to ensure an heir in the family line. But Judah did not keep his promise, and Tamar remained a childless widow. In her desperation, she dressed as a harlot and sat by the road she knew Judah would travel. He saw her, had sexual relations with her, and she conceived—though Judah did not know the woman was his daughter-in-law. Tamar was pregnant with twins; as the boys were being born, one put out his hand, and the midwife tied a scarlet thread around it, saying, "This one came out first" (Genesis 38:28 NKJV). Note the scarlet thread.

However, the baby pulled back his hand, and unexpectedly the other brother was born first. The surprised midwife said, "'How did you break through? This breach be upon you!' Therefore his name was called Perez" (Genesis 38:29b NKJV). Perez means breach or breakthrough. In Matthew 1:3 we read that Perez, the son of a woman posing as a harlot, was in the line of Jesus, the Messiah. Not only was Perez/Breakthrough (whose brother wore a red cord) in the lineage of Jesus, so was Rahab (who used a red cord, as we will see) a few generations later.

Judah's name means praise and it is through Judah's line that Jesus the Messiah would come. We've heard Jesus called The Lion of the Tribe of Judah, yet Judah was a sinful man; he thought his daughter-in-law was a prostitute, he slept with her, and she became pregnant with his twins. Even though Tamar had covered her face and Judah did not realize it was her he was having sexual relations with, he *did* believe he was having sexual relations with a prostitute, and he did know that was wrong in the eyes of God.

Yet, when Judah heard that Tamar was pregnant out of wedlock ("with child by harlotry" Genesis 28:24 NKJV), his instant reaction was that she be burned to death, according to the law. Quite the double standard: his disobeying the law was excusable, but her disobeying it was not.

When Tamar proved to Judah that the children she was carrying were his, he admitted his guilt and hypocrisy and owned the fact that

Tamar had been more righteous than he because he did not keep his promise to give her his son, Shelah, in marriage. According to the law, he should have given her Shelah to be her husband after her first two husbands (his other two sons) died, but he did not—effectively disobeying the law. Though the law did not condone sexual relations outside of marriage, Tamar *did* have a right to have a child through the line of Judah. Her methods were less than stellar, but she was within her legal rights and therefore, her actions more righteous than Judah's. God does not seem to judge with the same measures we tend to use.

Breaking Through In Prayer

In 1977 I lived with friends in Germany. Though they lived in Hamburg, their family home was in Berlin, and they wanted to show me what they could of their beautiful hometown. I was quite young then and certainly did not understand the full significance of what my eyes were seeing as we drove through East Germany on our way to West Berlin. The tension in the car and the sadness in Mutti and Papa's faces were enough to keep us all quiet as we drove on the one accessible highway to the one accessible city in all of East Germany: West Berlin.

These were the days of the Cold War and Russian occupation of East Germany and East Berlin. We passed through checkpoints along the way where we would be commanded to empty the car, the trunk, and, at one stop, even our suitcases. The authorities held a large mirror under the car to see if we trying to smuggle in anyone or anything; they were well aware of the damage one little breach could cause.

Upon arrival in West Berlin, we stayed with Papa's family and saw many of the sights of this remarkable city—beautiful even after the devastation of war. One of my favorite memories was attending the theatre where we saw a live production of *My Fair Lady* in German. We laughed and played and pretended all was well. And then we visited the Wall.

The Berlin Wall was erected overnight. It was originally made of barbed wired strung across Berlin, keeping the easterners in the east side and the westerners out—essentially making an island of West Berlin within East Germany. A heavily fortified wall was then built, with watch towers and army patrol cars that kept guard over the strip of "no man's land" on the east side of the wall, land in which IED's were buried. All of that added up to make escape from East Berlin into West Berlin nearly impossible. Yet we were told story after story of those in the east who tried to make their way to freedom in the west. Each night, at least one person risked the oppressed life they no longer found valuable to try to get to freedom. Some made it, but most did not.

The western side of the wall was covered with graffiti: words, phrases, poems of pain and suffering, drawings of death. The wall felt permanent, and the hopelessness on both sides was palpable.

I remember climbing to the top of a western lookout tower. To the east, everything appeared gray. I didn't see any sign of life except for the soldiers and their patrol dogs. To the west, I saw the green, flourishing, tree-lined streets of West Berlin, with its high-end shopping district and children playing in grassy parks. The contrast was overwhelming, and I felt overcome by grief. Tears began to fall down my face and I cried out to God to have mercy, to intervene, to come and make a way. Though I didn't have this language at that time, I prayed to the God of the Breakthrough to make a breach in the wall and set the East Berliners free.

Thankfully, that hateful Wall did come down in 1989, and I believe it was the result of the millions of prayers from as many people over the decades. I know the people of Germany prayed, but I also know that countless people like myself prayed for a nation not their own to be forgiven and set free.

Can you imagine what it felt like to break the first hole in that wall? Sometimes all it takes is one person breaking through, as with the twin sons of Tamar, to make a breach ready so others have access to a more abundant life.

Send in the Spies

The two Hebrew spies crossed into Canaan to look at the land God promised their people. Jericho was the first city they came to in the Promised Land, and once in Jericho, they stayed at Rahab's house. Whether she was an innkeeper or not, common courtesy and cultural norms would have dictated that she feed them with the delicious food available in Jericho. These men, who had only known manna and quail their entire lives, would surely have been treated to the taste of olives and garlic and the enticing, mouth-watering spices of Canaan. It must have been a strange night for the spies: to literally taste of the Promised Land but to also know that being discovered meant death. And it must have been a strange night for Rahab: to get a metaphorical taste of the God she yearned for while hearing her guests talk about Him.

The longing in Rahab's heart was for true love—love that could only be found in the heart of YWHW, the God of the spies who had come to visit. As she spoke with the spies that evening, an irreparable breach opened in her heart. I wonder whose heart was pounding harder, Rahab's or the spies? For the two things that make our adrenaline surge and our hearts beat fast are fear and love. Both the spies and Rahab had much to fear if they were found out, and both did what they did for the sake of love. Love risks in the midst of fear. We call that courage. It took courage and wisdom, strategy and faith for Rahab to receive the spies and know what to do—especially when she received a message from the King, telling her to send her visitors to report to him.

From what we read, Rahab was neither surprised nor intimidated by the message. If her standing in the city was such that authorities watched her house and alerted the king of her visitors, then we may assume this was not the first time she had been asked to send her guests to appear before the king, to explain their presence in Jericho. Scripture is very clear that the spies of Jericho knew who the Hebrew spies were and what they were about: to search out all the country. Rahab had waited for an opportunity to come in contact with someone who could lead her to the Hebrew God, so she took a big risk. When the king sent for the spies, she said she had not known where they were from and that they had already departed. But in fact, she hid them on her roof. Courage.

The only thing between Israel's promise and Rahab's longing was a wall--perhaps the largest, most impenetrable wall in history. On her own, Rahab could not escape. Yet even though she was confined within, she had a window. And through this window she had surely strained her eyes to see any sign of the people of God camped across the river nearby and calling out to Him, much like I did many years ago. Whether it is Rahab, you, or me, stepping into destiny will involve overcoming the walls that stand in the way. The only thing between you and your promise may be a wall.

The First Move

Someone has to make the first move. Whether stopped at a four-way intersection, working toward forgiveness and reconciliation in a relationship, or playing a game of chess, nothing happens until someone makes a move. Rahab had been watching for YWHW to make His move. She knew the Hebrews were coming and that the land would be theirs as God had promised it to them. In her eyes, the battle was of little consequence because God had declared the outcome to His children. She had heard the stories of the exploits of God as He called the Hebrews out of slavery and into Sonship. The testimony of His greatness confirmed that there was nothing this one true God could not, would not do—nowhere He would not go for love's sake. Her heart was confident that He who had heard His people's cries and rescued them from slavery in Egypt would be faithful to hear her cry and rescue her from her life of slavery in Jericho.

It All Adds Up

When Moses sent the twelve spies into Canaan, they came back with one branch that held a huge cluster of grapes:

> Then they came to the Valley of Eshcol, and there cut down a branch with one cluster of grapes; they carried it between two of them on a pole. They also brought some of the pomegranates and figs (Numbers 13:23).

They came back with one branch, laden with abundant fruit.

When Joshua sent two spies into Canaan, they came back with one woman with many family members:

> "Now the city shall be doomed by the Lord to destruction, it and all who are in it. Only Rahab the harlot shall live, she and all who are with her in the house, because she hid the messengers that we sent"....But Joshua had said to the two men who had spied out the country, "Go into the harlot's house, and from there bring out the woman and all that she has, as you swore to her." And the young men who had been spies went in and brought out Rahab, her father, her mother, her brothers and all that she had. So they brought out all her relatives and left them outside the camp of Israel....And Joshua spared Rahab the harlot, her father's household, and all that she had. So she dwells in Israel to this day, because she hid the messengers whom Joshua sent to spy out Jericho" (Joshua 6:17, 22-23, 25 NKJV).

A woman emerged from this breach, a woman whose reputation (because of her occupation) disqualified her for anything but judgment in the eyes of the law. But there is a Bridegroom who, from eternity, has patiently waited for His Bride, who saw in her someone He wanted in His family tree. Rahab, called the harlot, was the first bride to come out of the Promised Land, a fruitful bride who brought her family with her, whose future held more promise than she could know; a woman of virtue who saw through the wall of sin and shame, whose heart longed for the Bridegroom she had yet to meet.

Since before time began, it has always, always been about a Bridegroom and His Bride.

Questions for Consideration

In Luke 5:32, Jesus says He didn't come for the pure and upstanding; He came to call notorious sinners to rethink their lives and turn to God.

1. When you think of Rahab, Bathsheba, Judah, and Tamar, does your heart tell you one is less sinful or guilty than another? Whose sin is worse?
2. Is there anywhere in the Bible where we are commanded or commissioned to assess the measure of sin in a person? A region? A nation?
3. How did Jesus respond to those caught in sin? Has He changed?
4. What are we commissioned by Jesus to take into all the world? Is this just to those who seem to have it all together or to the Rahabs, Tamars and Judahs of today? How many people can you name who are longing for Jesus' rescue?
5. Spend whatever time is needed to listen to the Lord's heart for the lost. Be sure your heart is aligned with His, and rejoice in His kindness and the power of forgiveness.

A Blessing

Lord, create a breach in the wrong beliefs and attitudes in our hearts and minds! Enable us to escape the narrow confines of what religion and tradition have taught us are right, proper, pure and good, and show us Your standard of holiness, of beauty. Because YOUR standard is totally in line with your heart and Your Word.

I bless you, dear reader, to step into a wide space where the view is expansive and your range of vision is spirit-wide enough to truly see. In this new way of seeing others as God sees them, may you see yourself as heaven sees you, and may you grant others the same mercy He has granted you.

Chapter 4:
The Strategies

[Rahab:] Because I know all these things, this is my request: Since I have treated you kindly *and have protected you,* please promise me by the Eternal that you will do the same for my family. Give me some sign of good faith that *when you destroy this city* you will spare my father and mother, my brothers and sisters, and their families from death.

Spies: You had the power to turn us in, but you saved us. Now we will do the same for you. If you will promise not to tell anyone what we were doing here, *then you have our word:* we will treat you with kindness and faithfulness when the Eternal One gives us the land.

Since the rear wall of her house was actually part of the great city wall, she helped the men escape by simply lowering a rope for them from her window. *Before they climbed down,* she advised them to go into the mountains.

Rahab: *That way you won't be where the soldiers expect you to be. If you'll hide there for three days, the pursuers should have returned here by then and you can go back safely.*

Spies: We will keep the oath we have sworn to you, but only if you will follow these instructions: Gather all of your family here in this house, and tie this scarlet cord in the window where you let us down. If anyone goes out of the house and into the streets, then we *can't be responsible for what happens to them. They will be killed,* and their blood will be on their hands, not on ours. We will be responsible if anything should happen to anyone you gather in here. But remember—*all of this depends on you keeping your word. If you tell anyone our business, you will free us from our oath.*

Rahab: *Agreed.*

The men climbed down and escaped into the night, and she tied the scarlet cord in the window.—Joshua 2:12-21 Voice

Her husband has entrusted his heart to her, for she brings him the rich spoils of victory. All throughout her life she brings him what is good and not evil.

...

She gives out revelation-truth to feed others. She is like a trading ship bringing divine supplies from the merchant.

...

Her teachings are filled with wisdom and kindness as loving instruction pours from her lips. She watches over the ways of her household and meets every need they have. Proverbs 31:11-12, 14, 26-27 TPT

Taking Care Of Her Household

Traditionally, watchmen watch over a city or border, usually from a tower or wall. Their job is to keep an eye out for anyone approaching the city and to determine if they are friend or foe. A watchman cries out to the gatekeeper, letting him know if the gates to the city are to be opened or closed to the approaching party.

Rahab was not only physically positioned to be a watchman on the wall but she also, like the Proverbs 31 woman, watched over her household and family. As Rahab considered escape from the certain destruction coming to Jericho, she surely knew it would be easier to escape alone than with her family. Yet she was not willing to leave her family behind, so she watched and thought about how to include them in her plan.

It appears that she had thought through the oath she asked the spies to take. Whether or not she had, when push came to shove she was prepared to ask for a promise that would mean not only her own rescue but the salvation of her entire family. A true watchman never has only her own interests at heart but also the safety and protection of all in her care.

Securing the Future

Like Rahab, we secure our future by being prepared. The story of the ten virgins in Matthew 25:1-13 instructs us in the wisdom of planning ahead. When Jesus' disciples questioned Him about the signs of His coming, part of His response was this parable....

Ten virgins took their lamps and went out to meet the Bridegroom. How each of them wanted to be the bride! The five who were foolish took their lamps but did not take extra oil; they thought they knew when the Bridegroom would come and that it would be soon. After all, they were ready to go away with Him—surely He wouldn't delay. The five who were wise knew that sometimes we wait for our answer longer than we would choose, and they took extra oil with them. That way, when their lamps had burned up all the oil inside them, they could refill the lamps and still have light as they waited for His arrival. (Today this parable could be told using smart phones; be sure you not only have your phone fully charged, but also take the charger with you so the flashlight app is ready at a moment's notice!)

Time passed by as the Bridegroom was delayed, and all ten virgins fell asleep as they waited. Suddenly, at darkest midnight, they were awakened by a cry, "The Bridegroom is coming! Go out to meet Him!" You can imagine the bustle of those awakened from a deep sleep, trying desperately to wake up and get themselves ready and out the door. But it was dark, and they needed light to go out and see where to meet Him. The lamps of the foolish were going out and they asked the wise for some of their oil. The wise ones refused, knowing that if they gave away their oil, they, too, might run out, and then none of them would be able to go forward into their destiny as brides. So they told the foolish ones to go buy oil from those who sell it.

Sadly, as the foolish virgins hurried to the shop, the Bridegroom came and only those who were prepared became the Bride. When the others came back, they begged Him to open the door and let them in, but He refused, saying He did not even know who they were.

Jesus ends the parable with the admonition, "Watch therefore, for you know neither the day nor the hour in which the Son of Man is coming" (Matthew 25:13 NKJV).

What a sobering story.

And what heartache for those who neglected to prepare for the unexpected. Yet what a joyful celebration for those who had thought it through, realizing that someday their prince would come; though it took longer than anticipated, they would be ready and not miss him.

How long had Rahab waited for her moment of escape? We have no idea. But we do know she was wise, and when the time came, she was ready to see both herself and her family saved. The Proverbs 31 bride is one who watches over her house and family, just as Rahab, the bride-to-be, watched over hers.

The Importance of Our Words

I have learned a lot in the past few years about the importance of words. Sometimes the lessons have been painful and hard, but I got the message once I paid the price. In my book, *In Love, Where I Belong,* I write about my third-grade schoolteacher who tried to steal my voice by using, of all things, a sick game of words. I've learned that part of being set free from a fowler's snare is breaking free of the things spoken over me that are not true and do not define me. This includes words I have spoken over myself that do not stand in light of His face because they do not line up with how He sees me.

Many of us learn the lesson early on: "Keep your mouth shut and you'll be safe." While in some cases this is true and there is a time to speak and a time to be silent, overall this mindset has robbed the people of God of their willingness, courage, and resolve to speak up at all. God created with words, as He *is* the Word. We are created in His image and our words have power, too. I believe we are in a season when we—as the Bride of Christ—will find our voice once again to be the hope in the midst of chaos, light in the darkness, and truth in a world of lies.

Part of preparation is using the power of our words. Rahab's heart was filled with faith in this unknown God—this God of Israel who does wonders. It amazes me when I read the story of a woman who had only heard of Him secondhand yet who spoke with such faith and boldness to the Hebrew spies. She told *them* the stories of their own history with God, and the effect those stories had had on the people of Canaan. She sang her own song of deliverance to the spies when they stayed with her.

In Joshua 2:9-11, we can hear her faith in her own words, declared from her circumcised heart:

> "I know that the Lord has given you the land, that the terror of you has fallen on us, and that all the inhabitants of the land are fainthearted because of you. For we have heard how the Lord dried up the water of the Red Sea for you when you came out of Egypt, and what you did to the two kings of the Amorites who were on the other side of the Jordan, Sihon and Og, whom you utterly destroyed. And as soon as we heard these things, our hearts melted; neither did there remain any more courage in anyone because of you, for the Lord

your God, He is God in heaven above and on earth beneath (NKJV).

Remarkable. The voice of a prostitute who was trapped behind the walls of a wicked city, surrounded by the worship of false gods and all the sickness of soul that brings—her voice gave testimony of the glory and power of the Hebrew God. The original ten spies saw themselves like grasshoppers compared to the Canaanites—and believed the Canaanites saw them that way, too. But Rahab let these spies know the truth; the stories of Israelite deliverance from Egypt had been shared over and over in Canaan until the terror of Israel had caused all the people of Canaan to be frightened. The God of Israel is a God who does wonders, who intervenes with miracles for His people. Her declaration of faith sealed her fate; what bridegroom could resist such a passionate cry of love? The God named Love could not.

A Plan Larger Than Herself

Rahab's advice to the spies was simple and profound. She would lower them through her window, down the wall of Jericho with the red cord. They should go into the hills to avoid their pursuers and hide there for three days until the pursuers returned. After the third day, it would be safe for the spies to return to their base camp.

Rahab had a plan beyond herself. She hid the spies not once, but twice, making provision to protect her family and herself in the process. While the citizens of Jericho and all of Canaan looked at the Hebrews as the enemy, Rahab recognized them as the key to her future. It is one thing to be trapped in a sinful lifestyle; it is another to have sin lodge in your heart. Rahab may have been a prostitute in Jericho, but her soul longed to be a pure, valued woman outside its walls. Her occupation did not define her true, inner self. She shared with the spies her secret desire to know their God and the dream of counting herself among one of His children. As spies, they were trained to see and hear beyond the surface of what they were told. They apparently saw in Rahab a woman of valor. They now needed one another: the spies could not escape from Jericho without her help, nor could she without theirs. They promised to deliver Rahab and her family as she delivered the spies from Jericho.

I wonder if, as Rahab and the spies spoke that evening, they shared with her the story of Abraham being called by God out of an adulterous land? Of Sodom being destroyed but righteous Lot spared? Of the entire world being wiped out by a flood except for righteous Noah and his family? Did they fan the flame of her yearning for God by rehearsing again the stories of deliverance for which His fame had spread? Oh, to sit and soak in the hope that Truth brings! To know that "impossible" was not a word used by the Word! She not only "shared food from afar"—that is, shared the spiritual food of the testimonies she knew about YHWH—she also listened as the spies shared their own feast of His goodness with her.

We know that Rahab had flax on her rooftop. Flax means harvest, and harvest secures the future. Rahab covered the spies in flax not only to hide them but also to secure her destiny in freedom. She was a lady of sin in a city of sin. If she was indeed a spinner of yarn and a weaver of linen, it is possible she could have spun the bed sheets her trade was held upon. It is equally as probable she would have spun the scarlet cord that held and secured her future.

Positioned for Rescue

Having lowered the spies out through her window, all Rahab could do was watch and wait. The only strategies left to her were a window and a red cord. For the spies' departing instructions were that she tell no one their plans, to keep her family with her in the house at all times, to be ready at a moment's notice, and to hang a red cord in the window so they could find her in the midst of battle.

After we've done all we can do, all we can do is stand (Ephesians 6:13.) Rahab had done all she could do, and she surely stood in awe that this great God, whose love had tugged at her heart for so long, had chosen to send his people right to her door. In situations we know are out of our control we often still try to make a plan, working and reworking it in our minds. "Maybe if I do this, say that, look or act a certain way, then...." Our thoughts spin themselves into a tangled knot of anxiety if we forget that our only response is to stand and see the salvation of the Lord: He who excels in making a way where there is no way.

When Rahab hung the red cord, I wonder if she remembered the stories she'd been told about Passover in Egypt—how the angel of death had only passed over the doors anointed with the blood of sacrificed lambs. The first Passover was also for Egyptians who chose the God of Israel, and some did. In Jericho it was Rahab who chose Him and put the sign of belonging in her window so death would pass over her and her household. The red cord symbolized the blood of the Passover lamb, which symbolized Jesus: our way out of sin and into the arms of God.

Rahab's red cord speaks to us of Jesus' shed blood which saves, frees, rescues, heals, and releases us from our guilt and shame and separation from God caused by sin. Revelation 1:5 says Jesus is the One who loved us and washed us from our sins in His own blood. This blood of the Savior opens the way to the Father. This blood tears down all walls, however ancient or thick. This blood gives us total access to freedom.

Rahab's scarlet cord was a prophetic calling to a bloodline of destiny; its owner would play a great role in furthering His Kingdom on earth.

That cord hangs in the breach to remind us that no matter our past, all things are yet possible through Him for our future. He cleanses and makes clean and restores the years eaten by locusts—the devouring sins that can wipe out everything we hoped to become. Each of us can become part of the Bride of Christ, pure and spotless and free--even one named Rahab, the harlot.

Questions for Consideration

Our words matter. The Proverbs 31 woman is filled with wisdom and kindness as loving instruction pours from her lips. This bride watches—is a watchman—over her family, and she meets every need they have. In Proverbs 14:1, we read that every wise woman encourages and builds up her family, but a foolish woman, over time, tears hers down. And Proverbs 18:21 tells us that the tongue has the power to speak life or death.

1. Spin the thread your future hangs upon! What do you want the tapestry of your life to display? How do you see your future?
2. Name the threads you will need to use to create the future you want.
3. The best way to begin "spinning" those threads for your future is to speak out of your own mouth what you want. Write down a list of the things you long for and then speak them out often in prayer to the Lord.
4. Now consider what you want for the future of your family, community, state, nation, and other nations. Write down and speak those things in prayer and faith, and watch God work.

A Blessing

In every way you have spoken up and been silenced when you should not have been, may you experience God's mercy. In each instance you have spoken in anger or fear or frustration and caused a mess with your words, I declare crop failure over the seeds of destruction that took root. Over your bridal heart that just wants to declare the goodness and kindness of your Bridegroom, I speak release. Your words are powerful and they matter. May the blessings of the Lord bring a hundred-fold increase in your life.

I now bless you to use the vision of heaven you gained in our last exercise. Ask the Lord to show you what He sees for your future;

your children; your nation, and so on. Speak out this vision in faith and truth. Use Scripture to declare your destiny. Let faith build as you speak not what is, but the hope and future His word describes. Put your hiking shoes on and get ready to walk out of what has held you back and into courage!

CHAPTER 5:
THE WATCHERS

*T*he spies climbed into the mountains, just as Rahab had advised them, and they stayed for three days. During that time Jericho's soldiers combed the countryside and watched the road heading east looking for them. Finally they went back *to the city. So the two spies came down from their hiding place, crossed over the Jordan,* and returned to Joshua (son of Nun), where they told him what had happened.

Spies: There is no doubt that the Eternal One has delivered all the land *and its citizens* into our hands. Everyone there is scared to death about our coming.

...

Early the next morning, with Joshua leading them, the Israelites broke camp, left Shittim, and traveled to the eastern bank of the Jordan to set up camp again before crossing the river. Three days later, the leaders went through the camp and gave the Israelites their *marching* orders.

Leaders: *Tomorrow,* you will know it is time to go when you see the Levite priests carrying the covenant chest of the Eternal One, your God. Follow the chest so that you will know where you *'re supposed* *to go because you have not been this way before. But stay about half a mile away from it. Don't come any nearer than that as you march.*

***Joshua** (to the people):* Do all the ritual purifications and prepare yourselves because tomorrow the Eternal will show you wonders.

...

When the kings of the Amorites, who lived in the hills west of the Jordan, and the kings of the Canaanite cities *on the plain* by the sea heard how the Eternal had dried up the waters of the Jordan so the Israelites could cross, they were alarmed, and their courage failed at the thought of the *advancing* Israelites.—Joshua 2:22-24, 3:1-5, 5:1 Voice

She is not afraid of tribulation, for all her household is covered in the dual garments of righteousness and grace. Her clothing is beautifully knit together— a purple gown of exquisite linen.

...

Even her works of righteousness she does for the benefit of her enemies. Bold power and glorious majesty are wrapped around her as she laughs with joy over the latter days.—Proverbs 31:21-22, 24-25 TPT

A Whole Lot of Watching Going On

What a fascinating scenario unfolds in these verses. The tables have turned since the spies' first exploration into Canaan. Most of the original twelve spies saw themselves as too insignificant compared to the Canaanites; now the Canaanites are in fear of, not the Hebrews, but their amazing God. His reputation spread into every corner of the land and the people of Canaan now see themselves on the defensive. As the people prepared to cross the Jordan into their Promised Land, Joshua gave clear instructions how to proceed. He encouraged them that God is aware—and so is Joshua as their leader—that they have not done this before. This is a new day and requires a new level of listening, watching, and obeying. His charge ends with the reminder that God will do wonders for them—not just at some time in the distant future but the very next day.

Numerous times, the author of the Book of Joshua mentions events happening over the course of three days. This timeline provided a framework for the day of the Messiah; for three days He would lie in the grave, and then He would cross over the barrier of defeated death to life—everlasting life!

The spies crossed over the Jordan to get back to camp, then Joshua prepared the people to cross over and into Canaan. Interestingly, the very word "Hebrew" means "one who crosses over." Throughout the history of the Hebrew people, the Lord has led them to cross over barriers, enemy plans, and mindsets. Joshua was right when he said God was about to do wonders—plural.

Jericho watched for Israel to make its move. The waiting city likely didn't expect anything to happen soon; it was flood season. It made sense that the Israelite troops would have to wait for the waters to dissipate to they could advance. Rahab would have watched with anticipation and expectation, nerves taut, heart racing; the spies said to keep her family nearby, so surely they would be there any moment? If she is like most women I know, she checked the red cord multiple times a day, just to be sure it was still there and securely tied.

Watching On the Wall

One of the terms we use for "watching on the wall" is intercession. A watchman watches on the wall, and we've seen how Rahab watched Israel and looked for God from her window in the wall of the city.

To watch and then call out what one sees is part of what an intercessor does. Often the Lord will alert one or many of His children that something is not right; someone needs to pray. When we watch and listen, He shares His heart and secrets with us, which we then present back to Him in prayer.

Consider Abram at Sodom. We know that Abram saw the destruction about to be brought on that city, and he began talking to the Lord—interceding—on behalf of those who called Sodom and Gomorrah home. Though some people wonder whether Abram stopped too soon in his prayer, I stand in awe that he prayed at all. After all, if the people of the land were wiped out and all the land had a fresh start, didn't he stand to gain financially? There would be no competition for grazing his flocks in a land where water was precious. Yet he not only interceded, he did so on behalf of every righteous person who lived in the city—not just for his nephew and his family. It's a stunning and instructive story about intercession (see Genesis 18).

A number of years ago, I was given a word that I would work with people who lived at the foot of the wall. What in the world did that mean? I had no idea, so I did what one does: I held the word lightly and thanked the Lord that if this was true He, and not I, would make it happen. Since I had no idea what it meant, there wasn't much I could have done to try to make it happen, at any rate. About six years later, I was in a church in downtown Belfast, Northern Ireland, ministering to a group of ladies who have since become dear friends. Over the course of our informal discussion time, a lady of the evening walked in and began talking loudly, drawing attention to herself, using religious terms about Jesus in an effort, perhaps, to find a place of belonging. One of the women leaned over and said to me, "She lives just beside the church building here, right at the foot of the wall." Sure enough, the church was built against one of the many walls of separation in Belfast. Then I remembered my prayers and intercession in Berlin, Germany, and at the Great Wall in Beijing, China. Now here I was ministering at the foot of the wall in Belfast. Sometimes intercessors just need a wall to pray through.

Shut The Door and Open The Window

Back in the 1980s people loved to say, "When God shuts a door He opens a window." This line was meant to bring hope but it frustrated me. I prefer to just keep the door open! This seems to have happened in Jericho. "Now Jericho was securely shut up because of the children of Israel; none went out, and none came in" (Joshua 6:1 NKJV). This tells me that in a massive city surrounded by unimaginably huge walls, there was only one opening; only one breach; only one access--the window of Rahab. Something tells me Rahab kept her window open.

Isaiah 60:18 says: "you shall call your walls salvation and your gates praise" (NKJV). Though this refers to Jerusalem, a daughter with the heart of a child of the God of Israel had marked her place on the wall with not only a red cord but, more importantly, her prayers of faith. I like to think that the vibrations of her declarations of faith in the Hebrew God both weakened the walls that hemmed her in and reinforced her own home, her own dwelling space. That is one of the outcomes of intercession. Her home would not fall in judgment: it was saturated with her songs of deliverance.

Had Rahab ever known love? We are not told, but we do know that this great God everyone else was afraid of encountering was the One she was afraid of missing. The spies who came in His name met a need in her; they touched a tender place in the could-be calloused heart of a woman who had looked longingly out the window, over the wall, into distant freedom. She would make a way for Him to come to her rescue, she who would be in the scarlet bloodline of the Redeemer.

Perhaps before their first entrance into Jericho, the Israeli spies spent time watching the walls. Many travelers came into Jericho as the gates were being closed at sundown to find protection there for the night so the spies would have seen their opportunity to gain access. It would not have been too difficult to fit in with the flow of humanity pressing toward the gates. If Rahab kept her window open, it makes sense that they would have gone directly there, to the one place displaying a welcome. When the time for battle came, Canaanites ran into the city to hide behind the protection of Jericho's famed walls, not realizing the God of Israel walks right through walls.

The Way Across

It was flood season, and once again the children of Israel found themselves up against a river, this time the raging Jordan. An obstacle they could not, of their own devices, get across. The first time Pharoah's army had been in hot pursuit; this time they waited in obedience to see how Joshua and the Lord would do the undoable. These men were wanderers without land, cities, or well-equipped armies; yet so were their forefathers who had, with the Lord's help, defeated Pharoah's army and the kings of Sihon, Nophah, Medeba, and Dibon.

God created a wall of water as a breach to get Israel out of Egypt's path, and now He would do it again to lead them into Jericho. This symbolized not only the washing away of the shame of Egypt and the Israelites' consequent rebellion in the desert, it also foretold that Rahab, too, would be clean before Him. She who was watching and waiting for them to come to her rescue need only repent to become pure and spotless in His sight. God split apart the sea so they could walk across its dry bed, an act no more challenging to the Lord than walking upon water. Here's how it is recorded:

> The covenant chest of the Lord of all the earth will pass in front of you into the Jordan River.
>
> ...
>
> When the priests who bear the covenant chest of the Eternal, who is Lord over all the earth, step into the river, then you will see the waters of the Jordan stop as if behind a wall.

> So the people set out from their tents to cross the Jordan, with the priests carrying the covenant chest before them. During harvest time the Jordan is swollen, running over its banks; but when the priests stepped into the river's edge, the waters stopped, piling upstream at the city of Adam, near Zarethan, while the water flowing downstream toward the sea of the Arabah, the Dead Sea, ran out. Then the Israelites crossed the

Jordan opposite the city of Jericho, walking on dry land just as Moses had led their ancestors from Egypt. While the Israelites crossed on the dry riverbed, the priests who carried the covenant chest stood firmly in the middle of the Jordan until the last Israelite had crossed over.

...

On the western side of the Jordan stood about 40,000 men ready for battle, including fighters from the people of Reuben and Gad and the half-tribe of Manasseh who had crossed onto the plains of Jericho in the presence of the Eternal, as they had been commanded by Moses. —Joshua 3:11, 13-17; 4:12-13 Voice

All it took was a step of faith to cause the river to stop and back up to a place called Adam: a place of beginning. One step of faith and all the shame, reproach, and misery of Israel was rolled back like a scroll so that once again they could walk through a baptism of new beginnings into a new day. Rahab may have even seen this happen from her window.

Though archaeologists have thoroughly excavated the ancient site of Jericho, no one knows the exact location of Rahab's window in the wall. Wherever it was, I hope that she had a vantage point to see the troops of Israel coming toward her. Imagine what it would be like for her to see their approach; imagine the end to her sin, guilt, terror, and trauma. Imagine the sense of a new beginning.

Whether or not Rahab saw the Israelites approach, we can be certain the people who lived in Jericho and Canaan heard about the river crossing. It is not easy to keep secret the scene of a flooded river standing to attention as the Hebrew troops paraded through.

Those who did not get into Jericho before it shut itself up would have fled to the surrounding towns, spreading the news of the Hebrew's miraculous crossing—and also spreading the fear of the Israelite army and their God like wildfire. It could not have been long until the news was heralded far and wide both inside and outside the walls of Jericho: He has done it again! This God who defeated Pharaoh and made a mockery of the great and powerful Egypt has once again opened up a dry path through a very soggy floodplain.

What hope did Jericho have against such a Deity? What could they do against Living Water who commanded rivers and the rivers obeyed? They had heard the stories but now they had seen it for themselves. Rahab would have known for certain that this powerful, rescuing God would not forget or neglect to come for her. A God who can make walls out of water would find no problem taking down walls of stone. He had already dismantled the hard walls of her heart and made a way for her to be free.

Watching On the Wall

How grateful I am to serve a God who blesses, whose heart is not to smack His children into line in an effort to perfect us but whose heart is to walk with us in kindness. It is His kindness, after all, that leads us to repent. In walking with the Lord, we come to know His heart, His ways. It is out of this dynamic that intercession is birthed. As His representatives on earth, we are invited to intercede for and bless people, situations, and nations.

I'd like to comment on intercession before I continue. A key to fruitful intercession is to get quiet and listen to what He is saying. In His presence, seated with Him in heavenly places, you receive the strategies of third heaven, and pray those into earth. Once you feel you have heard His heart on a matter, be sure it lines up with scriptural principles. Praying the Scriptures is always a good way to intercede. If what you are praying does not line up with His word, repent and go back and spend time getting to know Him. A trustworthy friend who is a seasoned intercessor can be of great help if you are new to intercession.

Many years ago, Jim and I led a few trips into China to bring people from the US to see the challenges and greatness of that land and to bless the people we met there. On one trip, we had a couple that was, shall we say, challenging. On our first day in Beijing, we took the team to see some of the sights, including the Great Wall. We spent plenty of time climbing, taking photos. When it was time to leave, everyone was punctually on the tour bus except this particular couple. About the time we were ready to go look for them, they arrived and climbed aboard with smug faces. When we asked where they had been so long, they informed us they had come upon a Buddhist temple. The woman's next words chilled us to the bone: "But it's OK. We cursed that thing good!"

No! No! No! That land had born the weight of more than enough curses, and the Lord never, *ever* sent His people out to curse but to *bless*. In quiet prayer, Jim and I rebuked this couple's curse, stood in repentance for their foolish prayers by asking God for mercy, and blessed the monks. Did we bless Buddhism? No. Did we bless the deception? No. We blessed the monks and the people they served that they might have encounters with the one, true Jesus and come to know Him as Savior and Lord.

Rahab was trapped in so many situations that were not God's best for anyone. The last thing she needed was to be cursed. What she needed was an encounter with God, and that is what she received. Jericho's passions were dark, destructive. Jehovah's passions were for a Bride. For that Bride He would plan and wait and watch.

Questions for Consideration

When I read the biblical account of Rahab sharing her faith with the spies, I am faced with the question: do our stories of God's activity in our lives cause our enemies to fear? We don't read that Rahab had any God-stories (testimonies) of her own; she recounted to the spies what He had done for *their* families, not her own. Yet the stories that had been told around Jericho for years had caused a great fear of God and His people to come upon the residents of Jericho.

Remembering that our struggle is against evil spirits and not people:

1. Think of an example of God doing the impossible for someone you've heard about. Do you know this person or is it a story you've heard or read?

2. Acts 10:34 tells us that God is no respecter of persons. In light of that, think of a person who needs God's intervention as much as the person in question one. Does it seem possible that God will intervene for them?

3. What is a need you have that only God can fulfill?

4. God makes a way—in fact, Jesus *is* the Way. Do you believe He will come for and make a way for you? What is a first step you can take to agree with the way God is making for that need?

5. I began this chapter with this statement: 'Joshua encouraged them that God is aware—and so is Joshua as their leader—that they have not done this before. This is a new day and requires a new level of listening, watching, and obeying. His charge ends with the reminder that God will do wonders for them—not just at some time in the distant future but the very next day.' Dutch Sheets has stated that we, in 2018, have entered not just a new season but, in fact, a new era. In light of that, how might you prepare your life, schedule, mindset, expectations, prayer life, etc., to move forward expecting God to do wonders? What changes need to happen for the Body of Christ to be ready to receive those who are broken and lost in the spirit of adoption? How can we get ready to do what we've never done before?

A Blessing

With our western mindset, we tend to think of blessings as little more than wishes, and of curses as scary and forever. However, in the Hebrew language the opposite is true.

The Hebrew word *Klalah* is the word for curse and it has the connotation of that which is light in weight and therefore easily blown away, like chaff. At the name of Jesus, curses are blown away! However, the word for blessing is *Baruch* and it implies heaviness, weightiness—that which lasts; the blessings of God carry a substance that lasts. You're not only called to be free, you're blessed to be one who frees others.

This blessing is simple but weighty: be blessed as you bless others.

CHAPTER 6:
THE CIRCUMCISION

A t that time, the Eternal One commanded Joshua to make flint knives and reinstate the rite of circumcision for male Israelites. So Joshua made flint knives as he was told to do, and the Israelite males were circumcised at Gibeath-haaraloth. This is because all of the male Israelites who had fled from Egypt and all their soldiers who had fought so bravely had been circumcised, but they had died on the long journey. And those who had been born during the journey had not yet been circumcised....It was their children and grandchildren whom He raised up to receive that land instead. Joshua circumcised those sons and grandsons now because it had not been done previously. When they all had been circumcised, they remained in their camp until their wounds were healed. —Joshua 5:2-5, 7-8 The Voice

"There are many valiant and noble ones, but you have ascended above them all!"—Proverbs 31:29 TPT

Cycles and Circles

Ever feel like you're going around in circles? We all have, and not one of us likes the feeling. We are a people created to *be* and programmed to *do*. We like to have something to show for our efforts. Whether the "merry-go-round" syndrome shows up in a relationship, job, hobby, or the latest self-help program, going in circles frustrates us.

Imagine how the children of Israel felt after forty years of roaming in circles around the same wilderness. By that point, the original generation who had left Egypt had died and been buried in the sand; the ones who had received the judgment of not entering the Promised Land were now gone. Would this next generation, who had been born in the heat and danger of Sinai, now have to keep going in circles? Was there an end in sight or had the Lord forgotten His promise in His anger?

We know that God had not forgotten His people. In fact, the tedious cycle of wandering about on foot was soon to end, and His people were about to possess their Promised Land. We see a heart change that has taken place from one generation to the next. The first year out of Egypt, the former slaves complained of missing the onions they had enjoyed there. By year 40 – the time that we are considering here – the people were crying out for the bounty they had heard about that awaited them in Canaan. If you recall, the original twelve spies brought back not just grapes but figs and pomegranates. As this generation ate manna each day they would have heard their elders reminisce about the sweetness Canaan held in store, that they had tasted of only once. It's hard to stay satisfied with just bread when butter (milk) and honey are yours for the taking just over the Jordan! In yet another way we see a people longing and God's answer. Yet, though they would walk right in to possess the Promise and its bounty, their days of circling were not over. God was about to introduce a circling of a different nature: the covenant of circumcision.

Covenants Are Cut In Blood

Genesis 15 records the story of the covenant between God and Abram. In this covenant, the Lord promises two things to Abram: an heir from his own body from whom would come so many descendants they could not be numbered, and a land of promise he would inherit. Both promises seemed too impossible for Abram to believe them. God wanted to enter covenant with Abram, but He knew that Abram could not uphold his end of it, so He came to Abram in a vision. First, He had Abram bring sacrificial animals and cut them in two, placing the pieces opposite each other, thereby creating a bloody path on the soil between the animals. This was called The Walk Of Death or The Bloody Path, and it was a very serious matter to walk this path between the animals. By doing so, a person pledged, in blood, to keep the covenant being established. If they failed to keep it, what had happened to the animals would happen to them. Jeremiah 34 tells us that this covenant was cut before the Lord, and He took it very seriously. Because Abram could not fulfill or uphold such a pledge, God put Abram into a deep sleep, and His Presence appeared in the form of a firepot with a blazing torch that passed between the pieces of sacrificed animals. God had created Abram and knew that he, being human like you and me, would never be able to "do good enough", so God took the burden of the covenant upon Himself.

God is the only One who can never, and will never, break covenant. As George MacDonald wrote: "Paul says faith in God was counted righteousness before Moses was born. You may answer, Abraham was unjust in many things, and by no means a righteous man. True, he was not a righteous man in any complete sense. His righteousness would never have satisfied Paul; neither, you may be sure, did it satisfy Abraham. But his faith was nevertheless righteousness."[1]

You see, a covenant is not a contract. In today's world, we seldom talk about covenant, and we have lost much of the intrinsic meaning of this deeply powerful word. We know that marriage, baptism, and communion are the covenants of the Church. We don't enter a contract of marriage nor do we celebrate the contract of baptism or communion. They are covenants. But what does covenant mean?

---

[1] George McDonald Unspoken Sermons Third Series The Inheritance

Covenants require the shedding of blood. The Bible is a covenant book. Everything God has done is based on covenant and our relationship to Him. So what is the difference between a contract and a covenant? As you read the definitions, keep in mind marriage, communion, and baptism. It will soon become clear why we need to know what we have been invited into in God's Kingdom.

Definitions

A good place to start is with the definitions of each word. The *Merriam Webster Collegiate Dictionary*[2] tells that "contract" comes from a Latin root, meaning to draw together, to reduce in size.

Contract:
1. a binding agreement between two or more persons or parties, especially one legally enforceable
2. a business arrangement for the supply of goods or services at a fixed price
3. an order or arrangement for a hired assassin to kill someone
4. also, to contract, that is, to bring on oneself inadvertently as in incurring debts
5. to become affected with (as in pneumonia)
6. to limit, restrict
   Synonyms: shrink, condense, compress, constrict, deflate

Wow! That's not very life-giving or hopeful. Now, let's look at covenant, which comes from a Latin root meaning to agree.

Covenant:
1. a formal, solemn, and binding agreement; compact. (Compact is from a root that means to put together, to fasten.)
2. a written agreement or promise usually under seal between two or more parties
3. a pledge

---

2   10th Edition

Wow, again. Which would you choose for your marriage? for your walk with Father God? Thankfully, the blood of Jesus paid the blood covenant requirement of the Old Covenant law so that our blood does not have to be spilled to enter covenant with Him. Thank You, Lord, for the New Covenant in your blood that you offered for us.

The Covenant Of Circumcision

Wait. The word "wait" must rank near the top of our least favorite words, no matter the culture or era. No one likes to wait, and when we're waiting on a promise to be fulfilled, our inability to take matters into our own hands can lead to all sorts of inner turmoil. Poor Abram. Not only had the Lord entered covenant with him, He had promised him a son through Sarai, his wife. Many years passed after that promise, and no heir had been conceived or born. Nor was Abram living in the land of promise, and the hands of time kept ticking away. The Lord then appeared to Abram and once again reminded him of the covenant between them: "As for me, behold My covenant is with you, and you shall be a father of many nations." (Genesis 17:4 NKJV).

God restates the promise of possessing Canaan and then adds something interesting:

> "This is My covenant which you shall keep, between Me and
> you and your descendants after you: Every male child among
> you shall be circumcised, and you shall be circumcised in the
> flesh of your foreskins, and it shall be a sign of the covenant
> between Me and you" (Genesis 17:10-11).

God not only restated His promise of land and offspring to the waiting patriarch, He also imposed upon him and his descendants the sign of circumcision. This sign in the flesh of what God longed to do in men's hearts (Deuteronomy 10:16) became not only a covenant rite of the Jewish people but also signified the ability to reproduce and become a great nation according to the *Lord's* plan.

Part of God's covenant with the couple involved changing their names to reflect their new identity within that covenant. Abram and Sarai became Abraham and Sarah. Sarah conceived, and Abraham had a son of promise: Isaac.

Back To Jericho

Now a future generation of Abraham's promised offspring finds itself on the brink of the long-awaited Promised Land of Canaan. This generation had not known slavery in Egypt; except for Joshua and Caleb, all those that had were now dead. Those who were born in the years of wilderness wandering had not kept the covenant of circumcision—the cutting away God said would be the outward sign of their trust in and need for Him. When God spoke to Joshua and instructed him to circumcise the sons of Israel, Joshua quickly obeyed. Such a procedure made them even more vulnerable there in the shadow of Jericho's massive defenses. But their covenant God, their divine protection, was with them as they healed. It was important not only to obey the covenant but also to cut away the sin, disappointment, and trauma of the past season.

What a significant, powerful time this was. Don't miss what is happening here. An entire generation entered into a covenant—a cutting away, a new dedication, a setting aside (sanctification). The promise that seemed to take so long to come to pass was now here; they were beginning to live out the fulfillment of Abraham's covenant promise. Entering into the covenant of circumcision was vital for them to reproduce what the Lord desired for them in their new home of Canaan. They were circumcised in Sittim, the very place where they earlier had been guilty of harlotry (Numbers 25:1-3). I cannot overstate the importance of the symbolism of God cutting away their sin and shame.

Those going in to possess the promise have to pay their own price, have their own cutting away of sin, wrong thinking, and small faith. This generation had only known how to be nomads, and now they would settle in Canaan. Any weight of sin would hold them down and make advancement and fruitful settlement difficult if not impossible, so God symbolically rolled away their reproach (Joshua 5:10). The ancient covenant of circumcision was still fresh in its application and powerful in its impact as the people of God embarked on a new beginning.

The Power Of Symbolism

Talk about the timing of God. The Hebrews crossed the Jordan into the Promised Land on the first day of Passover. Their forefathers had experienced the power of the first Passover, which enabled them to leave Egypt. This new generation kept the Passover as they entered in to live in their promise. After forty years, a new generation of Hebrews, as numerous as the stars in the sky—like God had promised Abraham in an earlier covenant—had set foot in Canaan.

The fact that is was Passover means they were in the Hebraic calendar month of Nissan. The same month in which they walked freely out of Egypt is the month they would walk around Jericho's famed walls as a beachhead into their Promised Land. How exact is God's timing? Nissan is the month known as the month of praise, miracles; the month of redemption and to thank God for deliverance. It is the month of sound, and as we will soon see, they were told to march silently around Jericho until the Lord, through Joshua, gave the command to shout. His timing is beyond our ability to comprehend.

My dad served in the United States Army occupation troops at the end of the Korean War. He used to quip that the Army is all about "hurry up and wait". I guess some things never change. The Hebrew nation hurried across the Jordan, but once across, God's first instruction was to be circumcised—and wait. The men needed time to heal physically. They also needed to heal emotionally; the upcoming battle and victory would not be based on their strength but His.

I imagine that as they rested around the campfires, they told stories. After all, they had just walked across a dry river bottom to enter Canaan, so reminiscent of the stories they had heard as children from their parents who had walked across the Red Sea to escape Egypt. Surely the bookend stories of these miracles of God encouraged the soldiers who camped in sight of the intimidating walls of Jericho.

Here is Rahab's testimony to the spies *before* this miracle of the Jordan occurred:

> "We have heard how the Eternal held back the Red Sea so you could escape from Egypt on dry land and how you completely destroyed the Amorite kings, Sihon and Og – and their kingdoms – on the far side of the Jordan. As soon as this news reached us, our hearts melted like wax and none of us had an ounce of courage left. The Eternal One, your God, is truly God of the heavens above and the earth below." --Joshua 2:10-11 The Voice

Imagine the stories, the fear, and the gossip flying about in Jericho now. Who *is* this God of the Hebrews? And who—and what—can stop Him?

As if this were not enough, as the Hebrews camped and recovered, they also kept the Feast of Passover on the plains of Jericho. This was a collective remembrance of God delivering their fathers and grandfathers from Egypt by the application of the blood of a sacrificial lamb to the lintels and doorposts of their homes. Joshua and Caleb would have surely told tales of that time; they were the only two still alive from that time to tell.

As they celebrated the first Passover held in Canaan, I wonder if they also discussed what reproaches were rolled away: slavery, poverty, doubt, fear, unbelief, complaining, worshipping idols, sexual sin. The children of Israel had done it all, and now they were free of that past. What a setup to have compassion for Rahab and her family—to have faith that her reproach would be washed away by the application of blood as well. In the month of deliverance and redemption, God was about to show Himself strong on a prostitute's behalf. Truly, His ways are above and beyond our knowing.

But There's More

The very men who had just experienced circumcision were now instructed to circle Jericho. The battle plan of the Lord was to walk in circles—a pattern in which the Hebrews were well trained after their years in the wilderness. The root word of "circumcision" is circle. God sent His men to cut off, roll the reproach of Jericho's sin off the gateway to the land of promise. They were to walk in a circle around the city seven times, circumcising the sin, setting it into covenant alignment with God. Seven is the number of covenant and in fact, to make a covenant oath was to "seven oneself." Wow. Not one detail escapes the notice of our God.

Inside the city walls, Rahab waited, she whose heart had been circumcised by hearing the stories of this great God of the children of Israel. All that had gone before in her life—the sin, shame, depravity, terror, the self-loathing—was cut away as she believed the stories of God's greatness and put her full faith and future into His mighty hands. This formerly wanton woman entered the very lineage of Jesus because of circumcision—because of the blood shed that she, too, might enter into covenant and be known as part of Israel. Both the rescuers and the rescued had their sins cut away and stood in the mercy of the Passover Lamb. He who had rolled back the sea rolled back the reproach of His people as far back as Adam.

Our capacity for love and the Fruit of the Spirit all expand as we begin to see ourselves as our Father God does. When He looks at us through the shed blood of Jesus, He sees us as He longs for us to see ourselves: the cherished, desired, longed-for Bride. A new wineskin formed as a nation stepped into their inheritance and as a Canaanite woman stepped out of Jericho and into hers.

James 2:10 tells us that whoever keeps the whole law and yet stumbles in one point is guilty of all. Both male (the army) and female (Rahab) were sinners; as they all allowed the sword of the Word of God to cut away the past and the blood of the Lamb to wash away their sins, they became new creations. Religion tells you who *not* to love. Faith tells you who loves you. To this day, when Rahab's name is mentioned it is often with a disdainful, better-than-thou attitude of superiority by those with uncircumcised hearts who refuse to see this woman (sometimes any woman) as the chosen, pure, spotless Bride. When heaven speaks her name, it is with honor and respect due a well-loved daughter.

As the Bride of Christ, may we willingly submit to God any cycles that keep us in an emotional wilderness. May we allow Him to circumcise our hearts. The Message Bible translates Jeremiah 4:3-4a this way:

> Here's another Message from God the people of Judah and Jerusalem: "Plow your unplowed fields, but then don't plant weeds in the soil! Yes, circumcise your *lives* for God's sake. Plow your unplowed hearts, all you people of Judah and Jerusalem.

As we humble ourselves and allow Him to show us more clearly how full and complete is His forgiveness, how truly He has broken down every wall so we can be one pure, spotless Bride, we will be able to see the men and women who come after us walk out of oppression and into the freedom of a new day. It's a promise we've waited to cross into for long enough.

Questions for Consideration

1. Have you been feeling like you are going in circles? Is there a part of your heart that you need to let God circumcise?
2. For what have you been waiting, longing, a very long time? Rejoice that God knows and has a perfect time to come to your rescue. He's on His way.
3. How might God be asking you to become your most vulnerable on the brink of entering your promise? Are you willing to let Him

circumcise your heart in the very shadow of what seems most looming and impossible?

4. Once you begin advancing toward your promise, are you willing to surrender your need to understand the instructions for advancement? God told the Israelites to walk in circles. What seemingly strange thing might He be telling you that you don't understand? And are you willing to trust Him?

A Blessing

I bless you with a mind free of all its worries and a body free of all its pain (Ecclesiastes 11:10).

I bless you to be cleansed from everything that contaminates body and spirit (2 Corinthians 7:1).

I bless you with the desire to flee youthful passions and to instead pursue righteousness, faith, love, and peace. May you call on the Lord with a pure heart (2 Timothy 2:22).

And may the Lord grant you grace to submit to Him any cycles that keep you in an emotional wilderness, allowing Him to circumcise your heart so that you may enter your Promised Land free of the past. Amen and amen.

CHAPTER 7:
THE SOUND AND THE RESCUE

*J*oshua: *Shout! Shout! For the Eternal One has given you the city! 17 The city and all who are in it will be destroyed completely as an offering to Him, except for the prostitute Rahab and those who are with her in her house. Her life will be spared as a reward for sheltering our two spies.* —Joshua 6:16b-17 Voice

Who could ever find a wife like this one— she is a woman of strength and mighty valor! She's full of wealth and wisdom. The price paid for her was greater than many jewels.

...

She wraps herself in strength, might, and power in all her works.
—Proverbs 31:10, 17 TPT

The Fortress of Jericho

Jericho is considered not only one of the oldest cities in the world but also one of the geographically lowest. The city sits at nearly 800 feet below sea level in a region made lush and fertile from underground springs. Nearly everything about Jericho in Rahab's time made it a wealthy, vibrant city of trade. As the strongest fortress in Canaan, the city was built on the ruins of the previous city; instead of tearing down the old, they simply built upon it. Jericho sat upon a mound believed to be nearly seventy feet high. The city was also surrounded by a massive earthen rampart, reinforced by a stone retaining wall at its base. Onto this base rose two massive walls, each believed to be six feet thick; the outer wall was twelve to fifteen feet high, the inner wall sixteen to twenty feet high.

That is the imposing structure that loomed above the Israelites while they marched around it for seven days. In the natural, there was no way they could break through those walls. Good thing their Commander of Angel Armies was *supe*rnatural.

The Soles of Many Feet

Finally—finally!—the day of Israel's advancing arrived. Though the inhabitants of Jericho were frightened and unsure, at least now their enemy was making a move. The city could stage a counter attack once the Israelite's strategy became clear.

As for the Israelite soldiers, they must have been relieved that they could finally advance, although they, too, must have been wondering just what the battle plan was. And Rahab. After all the waiting and watching and wondering, she knew the soldiers were on the move toward the city. She must have wanted to grab the scarlet cord and wave it so they didn't miss or forget her! From our perspective all these years later, it is challenging to imagine Jericho's confusion and bewilderment while the soldiers just marched and returned to camp without firing an arrow or mounting a siege.

What were Rahab and her family thinking as Israel marched around and around without doing anything else? Day 1: Here they come! There they go. Day 2: Here they come! There they go. Tomorrow. Surely tomorrow....

This is the stuff of fairy tales, but it happened. And while it did, a family was trusting and hoping and hanging their very lives on the promise of two enemy spies. Talk about an unconventional rescue plan. Everything hung on the faithful power of this unconventional God.

The orders that the Lord—the Commander in Chief—gave to Joshua were strange at best:

The citizens of Jericho had barricaded themselves behind its high walls because of the Israelite forces. No one could get in or out.

Eternal One *(to Joshua): I have given Jericho, its king, and all its soldiers into your hands. Every day for the next six days, you will march once around the city walls with all your fighting force.*

...

Joshua gave the Israelites very strict instructions.

Joshua: *Don't yell or shout. Don't let your voice be heard until the day I tell you. And then I want you to shout with all your might* (Joshua 6:1-3, 10 Voice).

Ok, Lord. We'll march and then we'll shoot arrows, right? Throw spears? No? Just march...without even yelling a battle cry? What is going on?

These men had spent years learning to trust both God and Joshua implicitly; that trust was now put to the test. The Lord knew the effects that repeated, day-long marches around a city would have both on His men and on the mindset of the people of Jericho. God knew His men were just ending a time of healing rest. Each day they walked, they would have grown stronger, the forcefulness of their step shaking the ground, shaking the foundations of the walls and hearts of Jericho. And each day they walked without a shout, without a shot, the people of Jericho would be more and more confused.

Joshua told the soldiers to be silent as they marched; this not only conserved energy but also kept them from speaking any doubt or unbelief, from grumbling against the battle plan and against both their earthly commander Joshua and their heavenly commander, The

Lord. Besides, Joshua surely remembered the initial encouragement the Lord Himself gave him when he called him to lead the Hebrews: "Every place that the sole of your foot will tread upon I have given you, as I said to Moses" (Joshua 1:3 NKJV).

The Word gave a strange strategy: don't speak. Don't murmur as your parents did in the wilderness. Be faithful with what God tells you to do even when you don't understand it. Your parents and grandparents complained, and because of that, you have spent your whole lives walking around in circles in the wilderness. Now your circling has a purpose—trust Me. If you never speak your doubts aloud, they will die unborn.

Imagine the sound of soldiers marching day after day—the rhythmic sound of their footfalls in powerful cadence as the shofars sounded their war cry for them. As fear built in the surrounded city, imagine the courage it took for Rahab to stand in the window behind the red cord and watch as the soldiers continued to pass her by.

Take a Hike

Beginning in Luke 5:17, we read about an invalid man who had truly wonderful friends. When the man heard that the Healer was holding a service at a neighbor's home, he wanted to go. This was his big chance; maybe Jesus would heal *him*, too. His friends carried him on his bed to the house where Jesus was, but the house was crammed full with people—there was no room for a man lying on a bed. Not about to be deterred, the man's resourceful friends somehow managed to carry him through the crowd and up to the roof, where they pulled off enough roof tiles to lower their friend into the house. I wonder what the homeowner thought as tiles began falling onto those gathered below and he realized his roof was being breached? I especially wonder what Jesus thought. I suspect He smiled as He shared His heart about how the Father loved them all and had come to their rescue by sending Messiah. Did He just keep teaching as though nothing was happening, or did He stop and watch their faith in action?

Once the invalid man was lying on the floor, Jesus went right to the core of the longing of his heart by telling him his sins were forgiven. This stirred up a discussion among the religious people gathered there as they defended God's unique ability to forgive sins. How dare Jesus claim to be able to forgive sins? In classic Jesus style, He turned their religious argument back on them by healing the man with His words. In fact, He told the man to pick up his bed and walk. This act of walking was the punctuation at the end of the sentence as the healed man now held and controlled that which had essentially held him captive. When Jesus says you are forgiven, you are forgiven. When He says walk, even the lame can walk. At His word, go ahead and take another lap around your impossibility and watch it fall.

The Sound of the Shofar

For six days the army walked in circles around Jericho, circumcising the sin of the city from their inherited land. The soldiers leading the march carried the Ark of the Covenant, their earthly touch-point and assurance that God's presence was with them. Seven priests followed the Ark, carrying seven ram's horns—shofars. The number seven indicated that the Lord was in the midst of the battle with them.

Have you ever heard the blowing of a shofar? It is a trumpet made of a ram's horn, and it's penetrating, clarion call demands the attention of all who hear it. In the midst of the percussive marching, this riveting call to battle, to repentance, and to attention, would have pierced all who heard it. A friend of mine has made an intensive study of the shofar and how it was used for various occasions. He has come to the conclusion that the priests marching around Jericho would have made two distinct blasts on the horns. The initial blast is called the Tekiah, and it would have been blown for the six days they marched around Jericho once a day. The Tekiah is one long blast with a clear tone; it causes all resistance to God's presence to stop, and it establishes the boundary of what belongs to God. On the seventh day, on the seventh and final march around the city, came the Teruah blast. This alarm is a rapid series of nine short blasts declaring warfare and/or victory.

Psalm 47:5 speaks of the God of creation arising in Teruah: "God arises with the earsplitting shout of his people! God goes up with a trumpet blast! (Psalm 47:5 TPT) The sound of the shofar is the sound of covenant and it signifies God rising up to take His place. At this sound of the trumpet, the weight of His glory comes down. On the seventh day, the soldiers marched around the city seven times. Then came the sound of the Teruah, and Joshua told the soldiers to shout, for the Lord had given them the city. God's glory descended, and its weightiness caused the walls to collapse.

The Israelites had lifted their voices in agreement with God who had staked His claim in Jericho in Canaan. Everything that remained beyond the fallen walls—the gold and silver - and Rahab and her family—was now devoted to Him.

The Roar of Victory

The Hebrew army never fired a shot. They used the weapons of their voices and shouted with a roar of passion that had been building in them for generations—a roar of celebration that the centuries of waiting had now come to an end. The impossible had happened: they had taken the fortress of Jericho.

I think another shout was likely heard at the brink of victory: Rahab's shout—her cry for deliverance. It would have created a pressure from the inside of Jericho's wall. I see this symbol of the Bride of Christ crying out from inside Jericho, joining her voice to the collective shout of the warriors, who likewise compose the Bride of Christ. Their collective, passionate cry echoed God's cry and helped bring down the walls so sin and bondage could not continue to stand.

Once the walls fell, Rahab not only *walked out* of Jericho, she also *walked into* a new identity. As she left, she needed no makeup or finery of her former profession. It was *His* face alone she looked to, unashamed and free. She exchanged the clothing that advertised her trade for the robe of righteousness He provides. None of her words were recorded from the day of Jericho's fall. Some things are beyond the expression of words. Sometimes we just need to be still and give space to know that He is God and He is with us.

I love how God's words in Jeremiah 15: 20-21 read in The Message:

"Use words truly and well. Don't stoop to cheap whining. Then, but only then, you'll speak for me. Let your words change *them*. Don't change your words to suit them. I'll turn you into a steel wall, a thick steel wall, impregnable. They'll attack you but won't put a dent in you because I'm at your side, defending and delivering." God's Decree. "I'll deliver you from the grip of the wicked. I'll get you out of the clutch of the ruthless."

This is what the Lord did for Rahab. This is the truth the Proverbs 31 Bride lives in. This is the inheritance we, too, have received by His mercy.

Freedom

Some walls are built to keep people out, others to keep people in. It takes faith and courage to believe in a love so covenantly expansive that no wall can prevent it from reaching you.

Rahab's inheritance and destiny lay beyond a wall. As Love roamed about the earth seeking for a heart fully committed to receive, experience, and display love in purity, all it needed was an opening. A crack in one heart, a response to its knock, and Love came rushing in. That Love washed away the sin, failure, fear, and trauma of the past while keeping intact what could be used as foundation upon which to build a new life.

Walls could not keep Rahab in. Walls could not keep Love out. Having stepped out into the promise, she found its grace so expansive she could not see the end of it. There were no walls to this Love.

Walls of Our Own Making

We paint and decorate some walls, we spray graffiti on others. We build walls to bear the weight of a building or to partition spaces. I have climbed walls, sat on walls, and symbolically hit my head against one. I have walked on the Great Wall of China, leaned against small walls in rest, and torn out old walls with a hammer. Walls are important.

However, when sins of bitterness, fear, pride, or the like are left unchecked in our lives, they form a wall: a protective boundary we hide behind to keep God and others out and to keep ourselves within perceived safety. Jesus the Bridegroom is, without doubt, coming back for His Bride. She will look a lot like the Proverbs 31 woman whose life is described as full of valor and courage. The Bride will look like Rahab who overcame much and walked into freedom when God brought down the walls around her. The Bride will look a lot like you. When you repent and ask God to forgive you, your sins are forgiven, and the walls of separation between you and Him, male and female, slave and free are gone. No matter who you have been, where you have lived, or what you have done. As you allow Him to cut away all that stands in the way of freedom, you will stand up whole and start walking.

Questions for Consideration

Doubt is aborted if we do not give it voice. Take another lap around your impossibility, making furrows in the fertile ground of faith. In those furrows plant seeds that will produce the crop you want for yourself and your descendants.

1. There is a sound from heaven that opens a way to freedom. Have you heard that sound? How did the awareness of it come?
2. As God's people are remembering who and Whose they are, boldness is arising. Many are about to be saved and brought into the family of God. Ask the Lord to show you how prepared your heart is to love people you may not automatically be inclined to love. Give Him space and permission to call you into an expansive awareness of His love for each person, no matter what they have done or from what city or nation they come.
3. Rahab was asked to do specific things in order to be rescued during the chaos of battle. She did each of those things as instructed. What do you need to do to prepare for your deliverance? To help others walk into theirs?
4. What is God nudging you to do, think, and be, in order to help others come in to His expansive love?
5. There is also a sound within you that is ready to be released. As you let it go, walls that have held you captive will fall. Sound your trumpet! Shout your roar! And walk into the freedom Christ has made available.

A Blessing

I bless you with a voice of faith. May you use your words to speak destiny and hope into your life and the lives of those around you. I also bless you with the wisdom to be silent when God asks you to be silent. I bless you with a listening ear to hear what God wants to do in any given moment.

I bless you with patience when God asks you to camp out in the shadow of your promise, and I bless you with strength to start walking when He asks you to walk.

God is the God of the possible; may you trust His plan even if it makes no sense to the natural mind. Remember that He is the supernatural God. With Him, all things are possible.

Chapter 8:
The King and I

So Jericho was destroyed completely, burned to the ground except for the precious metals and iron and bronze vessels that were put into the treasury of the Eternal's house. But Joshua spared the life of Rahab the prostitute, all her family, and all she had because she was faithful to the spies he had sent, and she lived among the Israelites from that day on. —Joshua 6:24-25 Voice

Charm can mislead and beauty soon fades. The woman to be admired and praised is the woman who lives in the Fear-of-God. *Give her everything she deserves!* Festoon her life with praises! — Proverbs 31:30-31 The Message

The Rest of Rahab's Story

For I am jealous for you with godly jealousy. For I have betrothed you to one husband, that I may present you as a chaste virgin to Christ. —2 Corinthians 11:2 NKJV.

Salmon begot Boaz by Rahab, Boaz begot Obed by Ruth, Obed begot Jesse, and Jesse begot David the king. —Matthew 1:5-6a NKJV

"Do not fear, for you will not be ashamed; Neither be disgraced, for you will not be put to shame; For you will forget the shame of your youth, And will not remember the reproach of your widowhood anymore. For your Maker is your husband, *The Lord of hosts is* His name; *And your Redeemer is* the Holy One of Israel; *He is called the God of the whole earth.* —Isaiah 54:4-5 NKJV*

We have become familiar with the Christmas story as recorded in Matthew and Luke. Around Christmas, we often start reading in Matthew 1:18: "Now the birth of Jesus Christ was as follows...." (NKJV). We often skip the seventeen preceding verses even though they give us so much background and insight into this birth. What came before the *now* is vital to the whole story.

Both James and the author of Hebrews call Rahab by her old identity of harlot. Yet she is listed with great honor in the genealogy of Jesus. The fact that she was Boaz's mother lets us know she became Ruth's mother-in-law, though in the story of Ruth we only read of Naomi, her mother-in-law before she was widowed. The Book of James and the Book of Hebrews do not call Rahab a harlot as a slur but as a reminder that we serve the One true God who makes all things new and gives us identity in Him. No one is beyond His reach.

Hebrews 11:30-31 reads: "By faith the walls of Jericho fell down after they were encircled for seven days. By faith the harlot Rahab did not perish with those who did not believe, when she had received the spies with peace" (NKJV).

Rahab, a Gentile woman, welcomed the Hebrew spies in peace, with peace. In Ephesians 2, Paul writes to Gentiles about Jesus being our peace and breaking down the barrier. What barrier? The barrier between Gentile and Jew:

And He came and preached peace to you who were afar off and to those who were near. For through Him we both have access by one Spirit to the Father. Now, therefore, you are no longer strangers and foreigners, but fellow citizens with the saints and members of the household of God (Ephesians 2:17-19 NKJV).

Far and near, Jew and Gentile, then and now. This is not just a historical principle but an ever-present truth and reality—the reality in which Rahab lived.

In James, we read of Abraham, known as the father of faith, who lived out his faith in his actions, which justified him and made him righteous. And then: "Likewise, was not Rahab the harlot also justified by works when she received the messengers and sent them out another way?" (James 2:25 NKJV) Rahab, our heroine, is listed alongside Abraham. This is quite an endorsement. We marvel at how Abraham heard God call him out of a pagan evil society: He did the same with Rahab.

Abraham's descendants journeyed for generations to finally enter their Promised Land, and when they arrived, they found a woman of faith waiting for them. She was called out of the debauchery of Jericho but not called to leave the land. Rather, she was called to live in it as a display that God can redeem any person from anywhere if they are willing to believe, repent, and have faith.

The name Rahab means Overcomer. It takes Someone mighty and strong to overcome an overcomer. Her personal walls of self-defense and protection would have been thick and hard. Early on she learned to mistrust men. Was there One greater than a man who could speak true words of love and belonging? One whose very presence would make her feel safe, protected, valued, and honored? Jesus the Overcomer makes all things new and causes all who are His to be called overcomers—even fallen women. Even fallen men. The cry of Rahab's longing heart echoes through eternity and breaks down the walls of my own. We join her and countless others through the ages; we are the Bride who overcomes.

The Answer to My Cry

Interestingly, the longing I expressed at age eighteen was met by the man who would become my husband. I say "interestingly" because this deep longing of the soul does not require a human spouse to be fulfilled; Jesus *is* the Bridegroom of all who know Him.

It was 1978. Shortly after crying out to God to show me more of who He is, I was invited take part in a summer ministry group of young people. I had applied the previous year but had accepted an opportunity to spend time in Germany instead. At about the same time I cried out, a secretary at Lutheran Youth Encounter decided to look through files to see if there was anyone who might like to join the summer teams, and she found my application. When she called and invited me on board, I had three days to get to Amery, Wisconsin, to the camp where the training was being held.

When I arrived at the camp, I remember being overwhelmed by the concept of grace, which was a sure and steady theme throughout the two-week training. My heart expanded with the possibility of finding this God who seemed to be looking for me, and being with so many other young people who ached for Him as I did was balm to my soul.

One day, one of the pastors gave a lecture on the gifts of Holy Spirit and the working of signs, wonders, and miracles. He made it very clear that these things were confined to the Bible and we were not to let ourselves get swept up in such deceptions. As he was explaining that healing is not for today, a male voice from the back of the crowd asked, "Excuse me, how do you explain that a few weeks ago we prayed for a sick friend and he was instantly, miraculously healed?" The questioner had asked with a great, bold humility. The pastor had no response. He simply continued writing off prophecy, words of knowledge, speaking in tongues, and so on, warning us not to fall for them. But with each example the pastor mentioned, the voice from the back would respectfully ask for an explanation of the miracles he was seeing happen on a regular basis in his own circle of friends.

The pastor had been highly educated at the most expensive seminaries, but that voice knew Him who my heart loved! Some young man had met this Jesus, had been living a relationship with Holy Spirit, and knew the Father's heart. I had to meet him, but how? There were hundreds of us, and I couldn't see who had spoken.

Days went by, and I began to notice that many times when I turned around, the same young man would smile at me. Well, OK, we all smiled at each other, but I began to feel that this man's smile meant something more than hello. After a team campfire one evening, I headed toward the lodge to toss my pop can in the trash, and there sat this happy young man. I said something about not knowing his name but noticing that he always seemed to be there when I turned around.

He smiled again—a smile I've since become well acquainted with. "Hi," he said. "I'm Jim VanWinkle."

I recognized the voice I'd been wanting to meet.

We began talking, and Jim told me how Holy Spirit was moving in his area. In the late 70s, youth groups that met outside of church buildings were called Coffee Houses. There was no coffee, and usually the group met somewhere other than a house, but that was how these meetings were identified. We began to walk along the camp road as Jim told me story after story of the exploits of God he had experienced. We feasted on the testimonies of God's goodness until we suddenly realized that we'd walked all the way out the camp entrance road and back again, and we had missed curfew. All I could think of was my dad's reaction if I got thrown out of Bible camp for being with a boy!

I whispered that we'd have to try to sneak back into our respective cabins, when Jim reached out and took my arm, saying, "We can't go in, yet."

I thought, "If he tries to kiss me he'll undo everything he just said," so I'm sure the look on my face was defiant. Then, in the dark, I heard his voice say, "We need to pray together before we go, to thank God for this time and all He is doing in our lives."

Jim prayed, we parted ways and made it back to our bunks without incident. I fell asleep on a tear-soaked pillow that night, my heart knowing I had just encountered the two men my heart would always love.

Pursuing and encountering "the more" of God has been my story ever since that evening, and my name has been Mrs. Brenda VanWinkle for nearly four decades. Together, this three strand cord of Jesus, Jim and I has woven through life. We have parented together. We have pastored and mentored and served in the States, Southeast Asia, and Europe and now, we find ourselves in the role of grandparents. Our cord of connection has been tested and tried and is a bit frayed along the edges, but it is not easily broken because Jesus is the linking strand.

I like to think the cord with which we've woven our lives is scarlet.

The Goal

Love will always find the object of its affection. Jesus is looking for a Bride, a virtuous woman comprised of men and women who will run to Him—to freedom. He always finishes what He begins (see Philippians 1:6).

C.S. Lewis wrote[3]:

When I attempted...to describe our spiritual longing, I was omitting one of their most curious characteristics. We usually notice it just as the moment of vision dies away, as the music ends, or as the landscape loses the celestial light.... For a few minutes we have had the illusion of belonging to that world. Now we wake to find that it is no such thing. We have been mere spectators. Beauty has smiled, but not to welcome us; her face was turned in our direction, but not to see us. We have not been accepted, welcomed, or taken into the dance. We may go when we please, we may stay if we can: "Nobody marks us." A scientist may reply that since most of the things we call beautiful are inanimate, it is not very surprising that they take no notice of us. That, of course, is true. It is not the physical objects that I am speaking of, but that indescribable something of which they become for a moment the messengers. And part of the bitterness which mixes with the sweetness of that message is due to the fact that it so seldom seems to be a message intended for us, but rather something we have overheard. By bitterness I mean pain, not resentment. We should hardly dare to ask that any notice be taken of ourselves. But we pine. The sense that in this universe we are treated as strangers, the longing to be acknowledged, to meet with some response, to bridge some chasm that yawns between us and reality, is part of our inconsolable secret. And surely, from this point of view, the promise of glory, in the sense described, becomes highly relevant to our deep desire. For glory means good report with God, acceptance by God, response, acknowledgement, and welcome into the heart of things. The door on which we have been knocking all our lives will open at last.

This overwhelming love story we are invited into with Jesus is one of insatiable longing. It is a spiritual reality that the more you eat the hungrier you become in God's Kingdom. When we taste and see He is good it always "tastes like more." Thankfully, He is a generous Father and gives extravagantly to His children, even setting a table for us in the presence of our enemies, so there is no end to the journey of knowing Him.

Since childhood I have pictured God like a diamond with limitless facets of glory. I become enraptured by the beauty of one facet—say, His kindness—and I stare at and study and gaze on this facet and begin to become kind as He is kind. Then the diamond of His face turns toward me in a new angle, and gentleness lights up and displays itself. So I stare at and study and gaze on this facet of gentleness, becoming more gentle myself. In this way, I continue learning and emulating in-

---

3   Overheard Messages by CS Lewis. From *The Weight of Glory.* Page 355.

finite aspects of Who He is. My longing is both satisfied and increased with each dimension of this saving Lover of my soul.

The scarlet longing is fulfilled each moment we are in His presence, even as it continues to be an ache, a desire, a cry for more as the facets of His diamond-like glory are eternally revealed to His enraptured bride.

Without Jesus, we are each Rahab. Collectively in Him, we are all the Proverbs 31 woman. The prostitute who becomes the perfect bride is the wonder of the Bride for whom He will return. Rahab's passion for love met Jesus' passion for a Bride, and He tore down walls to reach her. God is still tearing down walls to bring forth His Bride.

All walls—even those as thick, formidable, and daunting as Jericho's—bow in the presence of Love.

The wonder of His goodness and might captured her soul. His love demolished her shame, regret, and rejection. Longing for Him displaced loathing of herself. The walls of her past fall away. It is *He* who is altogether lovely, not we. When we long for Him and are willing to count and pay the cost to be like Him, our spirit, soul, and body come into agreement and we are made whole. It is not our performance but our willing desire to know and be known by Him that causes us to be lovely—to be like Him so that we live in this truth: as He is in this world, so are we.

Brian Simmons wrote:

> Confidence grows when we see ourselves as He does, pure and lovely. Jesus is everything that righteousness stands for. He is the perfect example of manhood, perfection, grace and uprightness. Those who are upright in heart will see in Him their perfect model and spouse.[4]

Critical times require critical thinking. New and uncommon times require a new and uncommon ability to think more expansively than

---

4   *Song of Songs: The Journey of the Bride.* Loc 332.

we have thought before. To think outside the box. To love more lavishly, forgive more generously, accept more tenderly.

Listen to this speech of the Bridegroom from *The Passion Translation:*

O my beloved, you are lovely. When I see you in your beauty, I see a radiant city where we will dwell as one. More pleasing than any pleasure, more delightful than any delight, you have ravished my heart, stealing away my strength to resist you. Even hosts of angels stand in awe of you.

Turn your eyes from me; I can't take it anymore! I can't resist the passion of these eyes that I adore. Overpowered by a glance, my ravished heart—undone. Held captive by your love, *I am truly overcome!* For your undying devotion to me is the most yielded sacrifice (Song of Songs 6:4-5, emphasis mine).

The footnote for these verses tells us that the Hebrew word for "overcome" is *Rahab.*

This Scripture could then read, "You have Rahab'd My heart." Who would ever have thought this would be said of the harlot of Jericho? Who would have dared believe it would be said of you and me? As fellow members of the Proverbs 31 Bride, may we shout with joy:

Strength and honor are her clothing; She shall rejoice in time to come. Many daughters have done well, But you excel them all" (Proverbs 31:25, 29 NKJV).

Questions for Consideration

Rahab's story invites you to look at your future far beyond your lifetime. Her legacy includes Jesus; your legacy will include more than you know. Philippians 1:6 makes us gloriously aware that Jesus finishes what He begins. No one is a lost cause; none have fallen beyond the reach of His saving grace. No matter how soiled and dirty our lives may have become, His robe of righteousness won at the Cross makes us lovely.

1. What legacy do you hope to leave behind? If you've never thought about your legacy, can you start dreaming with God about it?
2. Do you feel disqualified to leave a legacy? If so, how might you claim Rahab's testimony for your own?
3. How can you partner with God in His plan for redemption on this earth? (Hint: if you don't know, ask Him.)

A Blessing

The Passion Translation of Psalm 91 presents a powerful description of the Bride reality in which Rahab and you and I live. Let these verses wash over you, deepening your awareness of His presence:

When you sit enthroned under the shadow of Shaddai, you are hidden in the strength of God Most High. He's the hope that holds me and the Stronghold to shelter me, the only God for me, and my great confidence. He will rescue you from every hidden trap of the enemy, and he will protect you from false accusation and any deadly curse. His massive arms are wrapped around you, protecting you. You can run under his covering of majesty and hide. His arms of faithfulness are a shield keeping you from harm. You will never worry about an attack of demonic forces at night nor have to fear a spirit of darkness coming against you. Don't fear a thing! Whether by night or by day, demonic danger will not trouble you, nor will the powers of evil launched against you. Even in a time of disaster, with thousands and thousands being killed, you will remain unscathed and unharmed. you will be a spectator as the wicked perish in judgment, for they will be paid back for what they have done! When we live our lives within the shadow of God Most High, our secret hiding place, we will always be shielded from harm. How then could evil prevail against us or disease infect us? God sends angels with special orders to protect you wherever you go, defending you from all harm. If you walk into a trap, they'll be there for you and keep you from stumbling. You'll even walk unharmed among the fiercest powers of darkness, trampling every one of them beneath your feet! For here is what the Lord has spoken to me: "Because you have delighted in me as my great lover, I will greatly protect you. I will set you in a high place, safe and secure before my face. I will answer your cry for help every time you pray, and you will find and feel my presence even in your time of pressure and trouble. I will be your glorious hero and give you a feast. You will be satisfied with a full life and with all that I do for you. For you will enjoy the fullness of my salvation!"

AFTERWARD

Writing this book challenged me, though I have carried its message in my heart for years. Amber's story in the prologue was the most difficult for me to take from heart to page. Everything about her challenged my religious understanding and righteous sensibilities, perhaps in the same way you have been challenged by seeing Rahab as a prototype of the Proverbs 31 woman. Such a challenge is a good thing; because behind every story there is a counter story. Yes, Rahab was a prostitute and yes, the Proverbs 31 woman has been a standard of virtue for longer than any of us can remember. Yet looking deeper, we have seen that when it comes to sin we are all Rahab. When it comes to mercy and forgiveness, Rahab is the Proverbs 31 ideal of the perfect, spotless Bride of Christ. When it comes to grace, so are you and I.

The reason Amber's story was so difficult for me to write is because her story is powerful, and I long to do her justice. Her life presents an example to us all and calls us to a deeper love and higher trust. I do not know what has happened to her in the years since we met. What I do know is that meeting her changed me forever, and I tell her story with great tenderness of heart and humility in the face of her courage.

I feel similar emotions for Rahab. Though the Bible does not tell us all the details of her life journey, what I do know makes her a heroine in my eyes. Neither Amber nor Rahab are who they appear at first meeting. There is far more to them than our initial perceptions, which is true of us all. They are rescued, redeemed, and fellow members of the Bride of Christ. Together with them and all who love and have loved Him through the ages, we ensure that the Proverbs 31 woman is complete.

We Called Her Amber

"Don't move. I'll be right back." Those were the last words Amber heard her mama speak as she sat rigid and afraid on the train station bench. The air was filled with unfamiliar noises and grownups dashing to catch their trains. Amber was three years old. As the youngest of six daughters of a poor peasant, she was dressed in hand-me-down clothing that was little more than rags by the time her siblings had all worn it before her. It was cold, and the rags were thin. Amber didn't know why mama had brought her to town or why they were here in this strange, scary place. Now mama was out of sight, lost in the crowd of people, and all Amber knew to do was sit still like she'd been told. Shivering and alone, she looked around in fear.

That fear was miniscule compared to the fear she was about to know.

Within moments, Amber's life changed. A soldier with an angry face picked her up and carried her away on the train. He took her to a child soldier camp which became her home. The soldier who purchased her from her parents was now her guardian. Her trainer. Her lover. No one else existed and no one else mattered: the sole purpose of her life was to please him and obey his every order.

By age five, Amber and the other children in the camp were experts with guns. When alarms and sirens and lights pierced their sleep in the middle of the night, they learned to jump out of bed and assemble their weapon in the allotted time. Failure to do so had serious repercussions, as did failure to do anything they were told.

Then came the raids—the raids the children were forced to enact, unspeakable raids of terror on villages at night. Amber and the other child soldiers—whose own innocence was long lost—were now forced to terrorize other innocent people. But no matter how perverse and severe the indoctrination or the punishment for disobedience, deep within her soul, Amber remembered another time, another life. She longed for it. This longing for freedom and truth became a heart cry that reached the ears of God.

By the time Amber was a teenager, the country of her birth began to ease its restrictions on foreign trade. Now and then, a Westerner would be seen in the town. And then a law was passed allowing aid workers to enter. One of these aid workers met Amber and her friends and told them about a man who could help them out of their guilt and anger and shame. This friend, whose name was Jesus, could make them clean on the inside, as though they'd never sinned. He was so powerful, He could even enable them to forgive the ones who had so deeply hurt and abused them. Desperately, these young women said yes to the offer of rescue and gave their hearts and lives to the One who had always been with them.

Amber and two of her friends then managed to escape to a neighboring country. How they escaped, I do not know. If bad news travels fast, good news travels faster, and the young women heard of a safe house in a certain town. Upon arriving, they were fed, given medical attention and prayer counseling as they slowly began putting their lives back together.

Shortly after this, but not knowing about it, Jim and I decided to visit this particular town as a break from work we were doing nearby. We arrived, checked into our scantly furnished hotel room, and fell on the bed ready for a nap when the phone rang. Only one person knew we were in town, so we knew who was calling—but we didn't know what she meant when she said, "Come over now. Someone here wants to meet you."

We had no idea that our worldview and compassion were about to expand. We arrived to find three young women—including Amber— who had escaped the camp and who now looked to us for comfort, prayer, encouragement, and belonging. We never knew the girls' real names, only the English ones they took for themselves upon escape.

We spent the next week praying, holding these young women, and singing to them as they wept. At one point, one of the girls curled up in a fetal position in my lap and screamed over and over, "Mama! Why? Why Mama? MAMA!!" We cried a lot. We even laughed at times. Though the pain in their lives was deeper than anything we could imagine, the reality of Christ in them—the hope of glory—caused their countenances to shine. They almost always had a smile on their faces or a song of praise on their lips. These precious young women who had every right to live with the heart of an orphan had found what it means to be adopted into the family of God. To be daughters of a good Father. To be part of the pure, spotless Bride of Christ.

After a few days, Amber told us her plan: She would go back to her family and her home. She knew she was being hunted by her captors, and she was more keenly aware than we were of the price she would pay if she were caught. But there was no stopping her for one reason: "My family does not know the love of Jesus; they have never heard His name. He is the most beautiful One in the world, and they must have an opportunity to hear about Him, to know Him as I do. If I don't go tell them, who will?"

The following week, Jim and I went to the border region to pray. We were traveling on a rickety bus on the top of a mountain as we headed for home. There was no road; the bus was making its way as best it could over rocks and through streams. At one point, our bus pulled into a ditch to make way for an oncoming bus headed the opposite direction. That's when we saw her: Amber was hanging out the window, waving wildly at us and grinning from ear to ear. We shouted out our love to one another and blew kisses across the ravine, tears flowing from each eye, expressing more than words ever could.

If I live to be one hundred, I will never forget Amber. I will remember the joy of her smile the last time I saw her. Her past no longer exists: Jesus' blood washed her clean. As one forgiven, she stands as a testimony of the power and possibilities made available through forgiveness. I am in awe of her bravery and humbled by her longing and passion to make the name of Jesus famous no matter the cost. She went from being a totally broken girl to being a Proverbs 31 bride, just like Rahab.

Many people had called her many things over the course of her captivity. We called her Amber, "the glory of God."

Questions for Consideration

"Bold power and glorious majesty are wrapped around her as she laughs with joy over the latter days" (Proverbs 31:25 NKJV).

1. Does this Scripture remind you of anyone you know? How does it reflect what I've written about Amber?
2. Do you believe this also about yourself? Is this how you see yourself?
3. Can you imagine the most notorious sinner you have ever heard or read about becoming this Bride? Why or why not?
4. How does God see you? If you don't know, ask Him to show you.

A Final Prayer

Dear Lord,

Thank you for removing the veils that have kept me from knowing you as you truly are. Thank you for replacing those unholy veils with the bridal veil that declares I am yours.

Thank you, Father, for the changes you have worked in me. Thank you for deepening my understanding and broadening my worldview. Thank you for increasing my ability to make mercy my default instead of judgment. I am grateful to you, Jesus, for seeking and saving the lost; thank you for seeking and saving me. Holy Spirit, I praise you for reminding me that the Bridegroom longs for me, and increasing my longing for Him. Place your seal upon my heart, a scarlet seal of longing, hope and remembrance. Amen.

EPILOGUE

No one's story is every fully written, for even after death, the reverberations of our choices go on. In writing the little bit I know of Amber's story, I realized a huge and important piece was missing for me: What happened once she returned home? Our concern, our fear, was that she had been caught by the authorities and killed. So when I would think of her it was with a large degree of sadness, yet also with the deep honor her story deserves.

A few months ago, a friend with whom we served in SE Asia connected with me via social media. We'd not been in touch for nine years, so have had much catching up to do about one another's lives and now grown-up families, and these stories made up our long-distance conversations. Until suddenly, just five days before this book went to the publisher, I thought to ask this friend about Amber, as she was the one who called us that beautiful, pivotal day to come minister to "someone who wants to meet you," and we met Amber and her friends. Rather than write it with my words, which would fail to express the deep emotion of her response, I will copy here, as it was sent to me, the correspondence containing what we learned about the fate of Amber.

The message I sent:

Do you know what became of Amber, the young woman from a nearby land? We met her when she and some friends came to your home in __ long ago. Her life and story imprinted itself in my heart and I've never forgotten to pray to the Lord about her. Her story, as I know it and journaled what I was told, has stayed with me and caused me to consider the life of a lady from the ancient past whose name was Rahab. I have spent years praying about these two and many like them, even including myself and my wrong ways. I have written a book about Rahab, and Amber's story is the one I use to open the book.

The response I received:

Yes, I *do* know Amber and love her dearly! She has become the *most amazing* woman, wife and mother to two children. She is now in charge of running the Sunday school in ___! Her husband is from this side of the border, plays in the worship band and works full time at an English school.

Amber—alive and well—a modern-day expression of one rescued out of darkness such as few of us have ever known, living and becoming the Proverbs 31 Bride of Christ! May we, like Amber and Rahab before her, be the conquerors we were created to be.

And may we never doubt the longing and ability of Jesus to rescue and save, ever again. After all, He came to seek and save the lost. Because from the beginning it has always, always been about the Bridegroom and His Bride.

But Jesus said, "The things which are impossible with men are possible with God."

Luke 18:27

"Behold, I am the Lord, the God of all flesh. Is there anything too hard for Me?"

Jeremiah 32:27

RESOURCE: JOSHUA 1-6

From The Voice Translation

1 Moses served the Eternal One *faithfully until the end of his days.* After his death, the Eternal singled out Joshua, the son of Nun, who had walked at the right hand of Moses *during the wilderness wanderings.*

Eternal One *(to Joshua)*: **²** Since My servant Moses is now dead, you and the Israelites must prepare to cross over the Jordan River to enter the land I have given you. **³** I will give you every place you walk, wherever your feet touch, just as I promised Moses. **⁴** From the *southern* deserts to *the northern mountains in* Lebanon, from the great Euphrates River *in the east*—including all the land of the Hittites—to the great *Mediterranean* Sea in the west, all of it is yours. **⁵** No one will be able to oppose you for as long as you live. I will be with you just as I was with Moses, and I will never fail or abandon you. **⁶** So be strong and courageous, for you will lead this people as they acquire and then divide the land I promised to their ancestors. **⁷** Always be strong and courageous, and always live by all of the law I gave to my servant Moses, never turning from it—even ever so slightly—so that you may succeed wherever you go. ⁸ Let *the words from* the book of the law be always on your lips. Meditate on them day and night so that you may be careful to live by all that is written in it. If you do, as you make your way *through this world,* you will prosper and always find success.

⁹ This is My command: be strong and courageous. Never be afraid or discouraged because *I am* your God, the Eternal One, *and I* will remain with you wherever you go.

[Joshua is following in the footsteps of the famous prophet, Moses, who led the people of Israel out of Egypt. It is a journey that will lead them where God wants them—in the lands He has long ago promised to the descendants of the patriarch Abraham. Although mighty people occupy the lands, God tells the Israelites that the land will be theirs, if they only believe. Joshua is reminded often enough of the wanderings in the desert following Moses. It's an intimidating thing to follow a legend, but the charge God gives Joshua also gives him what he needs to succeed: Be strong and courageous, and keep the words of God always in front of you. If you do those things, then you can't go wrong. And if you do those things, God says He will be with you.]

¹⁰ *When* Joshua *had heard God's commands, he* gathered the leaders of the people *of Israel* and gave them their instructions.

Joshua *(to all the leaders)*: ¹¹ Go through the camp and tell your people, "Gather whatever you need because in three days you will pass over the Jordan into the land the Eternal One, your God, has given you to possess. Soon it will be ours."

¹² Then Joshua spoke to *the leaders of* Reuben and Gad and the half-tribe of Manasseh.

Joshua: ¹³ Remember what Moses, the servant of the Eternal, told you: "The Eternal One, your God, is making a place for you to settle and will give you this land *as your own.*"

¹⁴ Your wives, your children, and your livestock will stay on this side of the Jordan in this land that Moses awarded you. But all of you who can fight must lead your brothers in battle formation over the Jordan and help them ¹⁵ until the Eternal gives them rest *from their*

enemies, as He has given rest to you. *Fight with them* until they, too, occupy the land your God, the Eternal One, is setting aside for them. Then you may *cross the Jordan again and* return to this land that Moses, His servant, has given you east of the Jordan and live here.

Leaders *(agreeing)*: ¹⁶ We will do all you have commanded, and we will go wherever you send us. ¹⁷ We will follow your orders just as we obeyed Moses in all he told us. May the Eternal One, your God, be with you as He was with Moses. ¹⁸ Anybody who rebels against or disobeys your words—all you command—will be put to death. Always be strong and courageous!

[Joshua has the promise of God that the Israelites will succeed, and the people have taken to his leadership with enthusiasm. They have begun well, and their faith will keep them strong. But in the conquest story they cannot expect God to do everything. A prayer from the Christian and Jewish traditions reminds us: Pray as if everything depends upon God; work as if everything depends upon us. Throughout the story of God's people, the partnership between human beings' faith and God's power leads to God's purposes being fulfilled in human lives.]

2 Then Joshua, the son of Nun, secretly sent two spies from Shittim *to the western side of the Jordan.*

Joshua: Go in, and see what you can find out about *the people in* that area. Pay special attention to *the city of* Jericho.

The men crossed the river, and when they entered *Jericho,* they stayed at the home of a prostitute named Rahab.

²⁻³ *Somehow* word reached the king of Jericho that Israelite spies had slipped into the area *and might be visiting Rahab.* That night the king sent *soldiers* to Rahab's house with a message.

Messengers: *The king commands you to* turn over the Israelite men who are staying with you because they are here to spy on all the land *and its defenses.*

⁴ But Rahab had already hidden the two spies *before she received the king's messengers.*

Rahab: It's true that two men have been to see me. But I didn't take the time to ask them where they came from. ⁵ *All I know is that* when it was getting dark outside and the gate was about to close, they got up and left. I don't know where they went from here. If you hurry, you might still catch up to them.

⁶ *She was lying,* because the two men lay where she had hidden them beneath the stalks of flax laid out on her roof.

⁷ The soldiers ordered the gate opened long enough for them to pass through; then the gate was closed. They took the road that went straight toward the narrowest parts of the Jordan, *which would be the easiest place for the spies to cross.*

⁸ But the two spies were still on Rahab's roof. She came up and found them awake.

Rahab: ⁹ I know the Eternal has given your people this land. Your coming has paralyzed us all with fear. ¹⁰ We have heard how the Eternal held back the Red Sea so you could escape from Egypt on dry land and how you completely destroyed the Amorite kings, Sihon and Og—*and their kingdoms*—on the far side of the Jordan. ¹¹ As soon as this news reached us, our hearts melted *like wax* and none of us had an ounce of courage left. The Eternal One, your God, is truly God of the heavens above and the earth below.

¹² Because I know all these things, *this is my request:* Since I have treated you kindly *and have protected you,* please promise me by the Eternal that you will do the same for my family. Give me some sign of good faith ¹³ that *when you destroy this city* you will spare my father and mother, my brothers and sisters, and their families from death.

Spies: ¹⁴ *You had the power to turn us in, but you saved us.* Now we will do the same for you. If you will promise not to tell anyone what we were doing here, *then you have our word:* we will treat you with kindness and faithfulness when the Eternal One gives us the land.

¹⁵ Since the rear wall of her house was actually part of the *great* city wall, she helped the men escape by simply lowering a rope for them from her window. ¹⁶ *Before they climbed down,* she advised them to go into the mountains.

Rahab: That way you won't be where the soldiers expect you to be. If you'll hide there for three days, the pursuers should have returned here by then and you can go back safely.

Spies: [17] We will keep the oath we have sworn to you, but [18] only if you will follow these instructions: Gather all of your family here in this house, and tie this scarlet cord in the window where you let us down. [19] If anyone goes out of the house and into the streets, then we can't be responsible for what happens to them. *They will be killed,* and their blood will be on their hands, not on ours. We will be responsible if anything should happen to anyone you gather in here. [20] But remember—*all of this depends on you keeping your word.* If you tell anyone our business, you will free us from our oath.

Rahab: [21] Agreed.

The men climbed down and escaped *into the night,* and she tied the scarlet cord in the window.

[The story of Rahab reminds us that throughout the history of Israel, unexpected people have stepped to the foreground to be used by God. Rahab is a woman in a male-centered world; and she is a prostitute, the kind of person we typically vilify. But if she doesn't rescue these men—and help them escape with the information they have gained—this first campaign in the land of Canaan will fail, and the larger outcome may be complicated—or worse. Her reward is life for herself and those she loves, which tells us that even in a war story like this one, God can be merciful.]

[22] The spies climbed into the mountains, *just as Rahab had advised them,* and they stayed for three days. During that time Jericho's soldiers combed the countryside and watched the road *heading east* looking for them. Finally they went back *to the city.* [23] So the two spies came down from their hiding place, crossed over *the Jordan,* and returned to Joshua (son of Nun), where they told him what had happened.

Spies: [24] There is no doubt that the Eternal One has delivered all the land *and its citizens* into our hands. Everyone there is scared to death about our coming.

3 Early the next morning, with Joshua leading them, the Israelites *broke camp,* left Shittim, and traveled to *the eastern bank of* the Jordan to set up camp again before crossing the river. ² Three days later, the leaders went through the camp ³⁻⁴ and gave the Israelites their *marching* orders.

[They camped where Balaam had come to curse Israel and where the men of Israel had gone after the Moabite prostitutes (Numbers 22–25).]

Leaders: *Tomorrow,* you will know it is time to go when you see the Levite priests carrying the covenant chest of the Eternal One, your God. Follow the chest so that you will know where you're supposed to go because you have not been this way before. But stay about half a mile away from it. Don't come any nearer than that *as you march.*

Joshua *(to the people)*: ⁵ Do all the ritual purifications and prepare yourselves because tomorrow the Eternal will show you wonders.

⁶ Joshua told the priests *from the tribe of Levi* to pick up the covenant chest and to walk in front of the people, so the priests lifted the chest and carried it to the front of the procession.

Eternal One *(to Joshua)*: ⁷ Today I *will do wonders that* will begin to show the Israelites that you have My special favor, that I am with you just as I was with Moses *before you.* ⁸ At your command, the priests will carry the covenant chest into the edge of the Jordan water and they are to stand there in the Jordan, waiting.

⁹ So Joshua called the Israelites together.

Joshua: Come closer, and hear what your God, the Eternal, has to say: ¹⁰ *Today* you will see a sign that the *one, true* living God is present among you, the God who will without doubt drive out all this land's inhabitants: Canaanites, Hittites, Hivites, Perizzites, Girgashites, Amorites, and Jebusites. ¹¹ The covenant chest of the Lord of all the earth will pass in front of you into the Jordan *River.* ¹² Now select twelve men, one from each tribe of Israel. ¹³ When the priests who bear the covenant chest of the Eternal, who is Lord over all the earth, step into the river, then you will see the waters of the Jordan stop as if behind a wall.

¹⁴ So the people set out from their tents to cross the Jordan, with the priests carrying the covenant chest before them. ¹⁵ During harvest time the Jordan is swollen, running over its banks; but when the priests stepped into the river's edge, ¹⁶⁻¹⁷ the waters stopped, piling upstream at the city of Adam, near Zarethan, while the water flowing downstream toward the sea of the Arabah, the Dead Sea, ran out. Then the Israelites crossed *the Jordan* opposite *the city of* Jericho, walking on dry land *just as Moses had led their ancestors from Egypt.* While the Israelites crossed on the dry riverbed, the priests who carried the covenant chest stood firmly in the middle of the Jordan until the last Israelite had crossed over.

4 When the last one had crossed the Jordan, the Eternal One spoke to Joshua.

Eternal One: ² Summon the twelve men you chose from the people, one representing each tribe, ³ and tell them to take twelve stones from the middle of the Jordan riverbed where the priests stand *with the covenant chest.* Tell them to carry these stones *this day,* and when the people make camp tonight, to lay them down.

⁴ Joshua *did just as He instructed and* summoned the twelve men, who had been chosen from the Israelites to represent the twelve tribes, ⁵ to give them instructions.

Joshua: Go back into the Jordan riverbed to the covenant chest of the Eternal your God, and each carry a stone upon your shoulder, (twelve stones for the twelve tribes of the Israelites) ⁶ so that we may build a memorial *of this day.* Someday when your children ask you, "Why are these stones piled up here?" ⁷ you will tell them how the waters of the Jordan parted as the covenant chest of the Eternal One crossed the river, and these stones will fix that memory for the Israelites forever.

[Memory is important in the Book of Joshua and in the stories that follow. When the people of Israel remember God's promises—and His goodness—good things happen. But when they forget, they turn to other things for meaning; they put their trust in other gods—money, power, position, and possessions. It's been a problem for the people of

God up to the present day, so these attempts to remember can remind us about God's great works. It has always been true that when God's people take their eyes off Him, they forget the lessons of the past. We honor God through our worship, and we are reminded of significant lessons learned when we praise Him.]

[8] The Israelites did as the Eternal commanded through Joshua. They carried twelve stones from the riverbed *that day,* one for each Israelite tribe, and laid them down that night when they made their camp. [9] Joshua also set up twelve stones in the middle of the Jordan where the priests who had carried the covenant chest stood, and the stones remain there to this day.

[10] The priests who carried the chest stood in the Jordan until all the people had hurried across, until all had been accomplished that the Eternal and Moses had commanded Joshua to tell the people.

[11] Only then, when all of the people had passed, did the priests bearing the chest of the Eternal cross over into the presence of the people.

[12-13] *On the western side of the Jordan* stood about 40,000 men ready for battle, including fighters from the people of Reuben and Gad and the half-tribe of Manasseh who had crossed onto the plains of Jericho in the presence of the Eternal, as they had been commanded by Moses. [14] That day the Eternal exalted Joshua in the eyes of the people, and they looked up to him (as they had looked up to Moses before him) for the rest of his life.

[15] Then the Eternal One told Joshua,

Eternal One: [16] Command the priests who are carrying the covenant chest to come out of the Jordan.

[17] Joshua gave the order.

[18] *As the people watched,* the priests carried the chest of the Eternal up out of the Jordan; and as soon as they had stepped out of the riverbed, the river was filled and overflowing, just as it had been before.

[19] The Israelites crossed the Jordan on the tenth day of the first month and camped at Gilgal on the eastern edge of Jericho. [20] This was

where Joshua set up the twelve stones from the Jordan riverbed. [21] He summoned the people of Israel.

Joshua: Someday your children will ask you, "What do these stones mean?" [22] And you will tell them, "Israel crossed the Jordan here on dry ground." [23] For the Eternal One, your God, dried up the waters of the Jordan until you crossed over (just as He held back the Red Sea for our parents until they crossed) [24] so that everyone on earth would know how powerful the Eternal is and so that you would reverence your God, the Eternal, forever.

5 When the kings of the Amorites, who lived *in the hills* west of the Jordan, and the kings of the Canaanite cities *on the plain* by the sea heard how the Eternal had dried up the waters of the Jordan so the Israelites could cross, they were alarmed, and their courage failed at the thought of the *advancing* Israelites.

[2] At that time, the Eternal One commanded Joshua to make flint knives and reinstate the rite of circumcision for male Israelites. [3] So Joshua made flint knives *as he was told to do,* and the Israelite males were circumcised at Gibeath-haaraloth.[4-5] This is because all of the male Israelites who had fled from Egypt and all their soldiers *who had fought so bravely* had been circumcised, but they had died on the *long* journey. And those who had been born during the journey had not yet been circumcised.

[Circumcision—the ritual removal of a male's foreskin, usually in infancy—is one of the ways God tells His people to distinguish themselves from those around them. This rite is carried out at this point in the story to reconfirm the Israelites' identity as God's people and to prepare them for the greatest celebration that marks them as God's people—the Passover—which commemorates God bringing them safely out of slavery in Egypt.]

[6] The Israelites had wandered in the wilderness for 40 years, and because they would not listen to the voice of the Eternal, God promised that none of the original community would live to enter the land He promised to their ancestors, a land flowing with milk and honey. [7] It was their children *and grandchildren* whom He raised up *to*

receive that land instead. Joshua circumcised those sons *and grandsons* now because it had not been done previously. ⁸ When they all had been circumcised, they remained in their camp until their wounds were healed. ⁹ *It was here, where they had piled up the stones, that* the Eternal spoke to Joshua.

Eternal One: On this day I have rolled away from you the shame of Egypt.

And the place is called Gilgal, *which means "circle of stones,"* even today.

¹⁰ While the Israelites were encamped at Gilgal on the desert plain *east* of Jericho, they celebrated their *first* Passover on the evening of the 14th of the month *in the land the Lord had promised them*; ¹¹ and the next day they ate some produce of the land, roasted grain, and flatbread. ¹² *Beginning after that Passover,* the Israelites were no longer fed with manna, *as they were in the desert.* From the day they ate from the new land, the manna ceased. From then on they ate *only* the crops of the land of Canaan.

¹³ Now when Joshua was traveling near *the city of* Jericho, he saw a man standing in front of him with a sword drawn and ready.

Joshua *(stepping toward him)*: Are you one of us, or are you one of our enemies?

The Man: ¹⁴ Neither; I am here now as commander of the Eternal's army.

Joshua *(falling to the ground)*: What is your command for your servant, my lord?

The Man: ¹⁵ Take off your sandals, for you are on holy ground.

So Joshua did.

6 The citizens of Jericho had barricaded themselves *behind its high walls* because of the Israelite forces. No one could get in or out.

Eternal One *(to Joshua)*: ² I have given Jericho, its king, and all its soldiers into your hands. ³ Every day for the next six days, you will march once around the city *walls* with all your fighting force. ⁴ Seven priests will go in front of the covenant chest, each carrying a trumpet made from a ram's horn. On the seventh day, you will march around the city *walls* seven times, and the priests will blow their trumpets. ⁵ When they play a long *final* blast, then all the people will give a mighty shout. The city walls will collapse *in front of you,* and all the Israelites will charge in *and take the city.*

⁶ So Joshua, the son of Nun, summoned the priests and instructed them.

Joshua: Take up the chest and have seven priests, each carrying a ram's horn trumpet, march in front of the covenant chest of the Eternal.

⁷ Then he gave orders to the people.

Joshua: March around the city with the fighting men marching ahead of the chest of the Eternal.

⁸⁻⁹ So they all proceeded as Joshua had commanded them. The fighting men led the way; the seven priests marched after them, blowing their horns continually in front of the covenant chest of the Eternal, and the rear guard followed behind.

¹⁰ Joshua gave the Israelites *very strict* instructions.

Joshua: Don't yell or shout. Don't let your voice be heard until the day I tell you. And then I want you to shout *with all your might.*

¹¹ So they circled the city once, carrying the covenant chest of the Eternal, and that night they returned to their camp. ¹² The next morning, Joshua rose early, the priests carried the chest of the Eternal, ¹³⁻¹⁴ and they all marched around the city *in exactly the same order as* they had the day before: the armed men, seven trumpeting priests, the chest of the Eternal, and the rear guard, all making one complete circuit *around the city with its great walls.* That night they returned to their camp, and the next four days proceeded just like the first two.

¹⁵ But on the seventh day, they rose with the sun and the procession marched around the city walls seven times; that was the only day they made seven circuits around the city *walls.* ¹⁶ After the seventh *and final* circuit, when the priests had raised a *mighty* noise on their trumpets, Joshua turned to the people.

Joshua: Shout! *Shout!* For the Eternal One has given you the city! ¹⁷ The city and all who are in it will be destroyed completely as an offering to Him, except for the prostitute Rahab and those who are with her in her house. Her life will be spared as a reward for sheltering our two spies.

¹⁸ Be sure to stay away from these things that He has devoted to complete destruction so that you won't be tempted to pick something up and carry it away. *Anyone who disobeys God in this matter* will bring destruction on all of us.

¹⁹ Any silver or gold, any bronze or iron vessels *should not be burned*; instead, they should be set aside for the Eternal's treasury.

²⁰ Then the people shouted, and the trumpets blasted. The noise of the voices and trumpets rose higher and higher, and the *thick* walls of Jericho collapsed, *just as God had promised. When the wall fell before them,* they rushed straight ahead and took the city, ²¹ killing everyone—all the men and women and children, all the cattle and livestock—with their swords.

Joshua *(to the two spies)*: ²² Go back to the house of the prostitute, and bring her out with all of those who have hidden there so that you can keep your word.

²³ So they set off *through the destruction,* found Rahab's house, and brought her and all she had—father and mother, brothers *and sisters,* and all her relatives—*out of the fallen city* to a place outside the camp of Israel.

²⁴ So Jericho was destroyed completely, burned to the ground except for the precious metals and iron and bronze vessels that were put into the treasury of the Eternal's house. ²⁵ But Joshua spared the life of Rahab the prostitute, all her family, and all she had because she was faithful to the spies he had sent, and she lived among the Israelites from that day on.

²⁶ *When the city lay in smoke and ashes,* Joshua pronounced a curse.

Joshua: May the Eternal curse anyone who ever rebuilds this city, this Jericho! If he lays new foundations, it will be over the grave of his firstborn; if he raises new gates, it will be to contain the corpse of his youngest!

[27] The Eternal One had helped Joshua, and his fame spread throughout the land.

Whether you want to purchase bulk copies of
The Scarlet Longing
or buy another book for a friend, get it now at:
www.abooksmart.com

If you have a book that you would like to publish,
contact Josh Babel, Publisher, at A Book's Mind:
josh@abooksmind.com.

www.abooksmind.com